The Activated Mind

Michael Hinkson

Introduction

"I've never had anybody explain things to me like this before."

"Why hasn't anyone else ever shown me this before?"

These are comments that I regularly hear from new clients during our first session. They typically come from people who have been involved in treatment, on and off, for the past ten to twenty years. Reactions like this occur because I define psychotherapy in a way that they've never heard before and it makes complete sense to them. I've witnessed dramatic transformations unfold as I've watched my clients apply the process. It's very gratifying to see people, who have struggled for so long, finally get the results that they have always desired.

As a psychotherapist, you tend to live your career in a bubble. Unless you work in a team treatment model, which generally only exists in residential or hospital settings, you work alone. I have worked in large outpatient clinics, with up to thirty therapists in the office, for most of my career. Day after day, for years, I have worked with colleagues in offices right next to mine, and I have had no idea how they approach therapy with their clients. It's very easy to conclude that everyone else basically practices psychotherapy the same way. However, as I continued to hear increasing comments like the ones noted above, I began thinking that perhaps the way I approach psychotherapy is more unique than I'd originally believed.

It's very sad when I have a client who is in their late forties or early fifties, tell me, with tears in their eyes, that they wish they had been exposed to this type of treatment twenty years ago. It has been these experiences that have motivated me to capture, as clearly as possible, what takes place in my sessions with clients.

Contained in this work is what I believe to be the most crucial elements of successful psychotherapy. This book is dedicated to all those I have worked with in treatment and to all who struggle with fear – the underlying cause of most mental health issues. My hope is that what follows will help you to make the changes you have always wanted in your life.

Michael Hinkson MA, LPC

Chapter 1: The Structure and Development of the Mind

It is important to understand how the mind is structured and how it works. There are two levels of the mind, the conscious and the subconscious. The conscious part of the mind is connected directly to the senses. It can only focus on one thing at a time. It can distinguish person, place, time, right, wrong, true and false. The conscious mind has the ability to operate with logic and reasoning. Its job is to function as our filter of reality and our experiences in life. The conscious mind is supposed to take information, apply correct perception, and decide to either accept or reject information based on validity. This part of the mind turns on and off. It's on when we are awake and off when we sleep because it's directly tied to the senses. When the senses are shut off, as they are when we are sleeping, it turns off. The conscious mind is bombarded by tens of thousands of pieces of sensory information each day and can become easily distracted. It also gets distracted by unresolved problems and issues that we are dealing with. Day dreaming is a concept that most people are familiar with and illustrates how the conscious mind's attention will drift away from its here and now focus and onto another subject. When we are day dreaming, it's preoccupied with other pieces of information that are not part of what we should be focusing on at the moment. A good example of this is an experience everyone has had who drives a vehicle. You are driving along and your conscious mind becomes engrossed in something else not connected with driving. Maybe you had an argument with your spouse before leaving for work and now you are playing it back in your mind. Whatever it may be, it is some type of issue that is more important to you at the moment than driving. When your conscious awareness finally snaps back to driving, you realize that you have just gone a half a mile and you don't remember any of it. How were you able to drive safely? You were able to because your subconscious mind took over the function of driving while your conscious mind was distracted. Driving is an action that has been done so many times that it has been habituated. This means that we don't have to consciously think about it to do it anymore. This is an example of the conscious and subconscious minds working together.

In your imagination, think of the most massive library you can envision in your mind. This is the subconscious mind. It stores all of our experiences, learning and memories. If you've ever seen a Rubik's Cube, this is exactly how the subconscious mind is structured. It isn't dependent on our senses to receive information. The subconscious mind takes in everything that is happening around us. In comparison, the conscious mind is limited in scope. Have you ever read or typed on a computer and tried to listen to someone talking on the television at the same time? It's not possible because of the limited focus of the conscious mind. To understand what is being said on the television, you have to stop what you are doing on the computer and turn your sense of hearing to the words being spoken. If you wish to resume your work on the computer, you have to turn your senses away from the television and back on the computer. However, your subconscious mind has received and stored everything in the memory.

The subconscious mind does not distinguish right, wrong, true, false, time, place or person. This is a very important point that will be returned to later on. Its only job is to receive and store information according to importance in memory compartments. How does it distinguish importance? The subconscious mind determines importance solely by pure repetition. This means that if a thought, experience, belief or statement is repeated enough times, it will automatically validate it and believe it to be true. This is another very important concept to understand. What happens if a person tells a lie long enough? There will come a point in time when they fully believe the lie to be true and will have lost any ability to remember that it was false to begin with. This is how a delusionary system is built in the mind that the person now operates with that will eventually cause all sorts of problems for them. The subconscious mind never turns off because it's not directly tied to the senses. It's on 24/7 and is the source of dreams and nightmares when we are asleep. The subconscious mind is on, and fully functioning, even when we are in our mother's womb. The conscious mind is not. In fact, the conscious mind is not fully functioning until we enter late adolescence, or even early adulthood. Overtime, with the learning that comes from experience, the conscious mind eventually matures to the point where it can fully assume its leadership role. This is another very important concept that we will return to later on.

The information we use and rely on the most in our lives is stored in the compartments on the very top level of the subconscious mind. Things like family, friends, school, work, finances, religion, driving, favorite foods, exercise, hobbies, leisure activities, etc. The most critical information that exists in the whole subconscious realm is stored in the very middle of that top level. The belief systems stored here determine our mood structure, our perception of reality, how our senses are directed and, ultimately, our actions in life. These two belief systems are our self-view and our world-view, which includes our view of people.

These belief systems become our life goal and life directive. They are formed as a direct result of our life experiences, especially those that occur in our childhood. These two belief systems are either positive or negative. They will never form with one being positive and one negative. The self-view and world-view are intimately linked. A child's self-view is completely dependent on their world-view for its formation. In the early development of the mind, the world-view forms first and then the self-view second. The world-view of a child is directly shaped by the experiences the parents provide for them. If those experiences are predominantly negative, then the world view will be negative and the child will conclude their self-view based on this. Because the subconscious mind is already operating when the baby is in the womb, these belief systems are forming before birth. After birth, the brain is developing at its most rapid rate during early childhood. Early childhood experiences are responsible for the learning that becomes integrated into the subconscious mind that determines the quality of the rest of our lives. There is absolute truth in this statement:

What we are is the result of what we think.

Or, with a little more detail:

The quality of our lives is the direct reflection of the quality of our belief systems.

For any person, it is crucial to find out what the status of these two belief systems is. This is not as easy as you would think. Because the conscious mind is not fully developed and mature enough to function the way it is supposed to until late adolescence or early adulthood, the belief system development bypasses the conscious filter. If the belief systems are shaped positive, this does not present a problem. However, if they form negatively, then we are destined for serious problems.

To review, the conscious mind is the guardian, the filter, the judge, the gardener, the teacher and the parent. Because it operates with logic, it's designed to be the leader and in full control of our decision making process.

The conscious mind knows right from wrong and true from false, so it's built to deal with experience on these terms. But, it can only serve this role when it is old enough and mature enough to take the lead. This is why the quality of parenting is so vital to the development of a child's mind. The mind is the most important feature of a human being to be developed. Now, remember how the subconscious mind works. It takes in everything without regard for whether it is good or bad information. In addition, if an experience repeats enough times, even if it is negative in nature, the subconscious mind will automatically assume it's true. In early childhood, the child's subconscious mind is absorbing experiences at a rapid pace. The developing mind is processing this new information at a staggering rate, so the parent needs to protect what the child is exposed to. Those absolutely critical belief systems are forming every hour of every day. The child's predominant world view when the belief systems are forming is that which the parents provide. Let me reiterate this statement because it is so important.

The parents provide the quality of experiences that will determine the quality of their child's mind and, therefore, the quality of their child's life as they grow older, even as an adult.

Until the child's conscious mind is ready to do its job, the parents act as the child's conscious mind. The parents are supposed to provide basic needs, safety, soothe, calm, provide logic, teach about the world, protect the child's experiences, provide correct learning from experiences, create positive experiences and fill the child with love, value, purpose and meaning. If the parents fulfill their role, then the child will grow up with a healthy view of the world, people and themselves. The parents' right actions will provide the framework for, and accelerate, the conscious mind's growth and development. If the parents don't fulfill their role, and the quality of a child's world is predominantly negative, then their belief about the world and themselves will become negative. If a child is shown, or told, that they are dumb and stupid enough times, they will come to believe that they are dumb and stupid, will feel dumb and stupid, and then will act dumb and stupid. The child's subconscious mind will have integrated as truth a belief that is completely false. However, the subconscious mind does not filter true and false, and now believes this to be the child's life goal- to be dumb and stupid. As long as this self-view continues to remain integrated into the subconscious mind, the child will continue to act on script, even into adulthood, unless the conscious mind awakens later on and corrects the false learning.

This is how negative belief systems form and bypass the conscious mind. They become integrated into the subconscious mind, and then immediately start steering the child's life into repeated cycles of problems and misery. When I say integrated, I mean that the belief systems become habituated which means that we don't have to consciously think about them in order to act on them. They just run on automatic pilot. This is how, later on in life, a person can think they are positive minded but, in actuality, are anything but positive. Their conscious mind has no idea what is actually going on down in the subconscious level. Anyone who has repeated patterns of chronic mood disturbance, problematic relationships, and failure to achieve goals, has to look into their subconscious mind because these cycles are evidence that their belief systems are negative.

To review, the quality of parenting is directly responsible for the quality of a child's mind. It is the dominant factor. However, early educational and social experiences also can heavily factor in. Parents can be doing their best to fill their child's mind with positive experiences, but a child can struggle learning in school, or have poor social experiences such as bullying. These negative experiences, if severe enough and repeated enough, can turn a child's previously positive forming belief systems negative. However, the parental response is of utmost importance. Parents who intervene quickly and effectively on these issues can stop the belief systems from turning negative. It's crucial that parents model to their children how to appropriately resolve problems. Critical in a child's belief system, or anyone's for that matter, is having the confidence to correctly handle problems when they arise. The foundation of a powerful self-image is being able to look at all problems and obstacles as opportunities to get stronger, having the belief that every problem has a solution, and that the ability to find resolution lies within us. Strong, quality parenting can compensate for any negative experience a child may run into outside of the household.

An important point has been raised in the previous discussion. Belief systems, once formed, are not permanent and can be changed. If not awake and consciously vigilant, a person, whose belief systems are positive, can enter a period in their life of negative experience and they will turn negative. It only takes **three to four weeks** of repetitive negative thinking, triggered by adverse experiences, for the subconscious mind to integrate this thinking as a truth. Negative life experiences can cause us to initially think badly about ourselves and our world. If this thinking continues in a repetitive pattern, the subconscious mind will take this as a directive to remove the previous positive belief systems and insert the negative ones. And, as noted above, it only takes a matter of weeks for this to happen, not months or years. This is why it's so important that we watch our thought process and never allow adverse experiences in life to cause us to start thinking in negative terms about ourselves and the world. Even one experience, if powerful enough, can trigger this change.

An example of this is an individual who suffers a terrible car accident. A car accident occurs in a split second. In that instant, a person's world view and, specifically, their view of driving, can be turned from positive to negative if traumatic enough. Before the accident, driving was believed to be safe and secure. There was not an ounce of thought connected to driving being dangerous, or potentially life threatening. After the accident, the world is now a dangerous place where horrible things can happen, especially if you drive. In fact, you could die. The person now can't drive and has terrible panic attacks in a car, even as a passenger. This is how fast the subconscious mind will grab onto, and integrate, a negative belief system if the adverse event is strong enough. If not addressed immediately, the fear of driving will slowly, but surely, spread and invade other areas of the person's life. The good news is that this negative learning, no matter how traumatic, can be replaced by the positive opposite belief. I have worked with many accident victims over the years and they have been able to return to driving independently. Once a person wakes up to the presence of negative belief systems residing in their subconscious mind, they can begin the process of positive change. After all, we are just dealing with learning. Anything that is learned, can be unlearned, and new learning can be put in its place.

The following charts illustrate the structure of the mind. They are constructed in two dimensional form which is how I present them on a white board in session. It's easier for me to draw them this way and a much simpler visual for the client to understand.

The Structure of the Mind

*← ***Conscious Mind***

Subconscious Mind

Completely functional when we are in our mother's womb.

Acts like a library by receiving and storing information.

Built to follow the conscious mind's direction.

Automatically validates any information if repeated enough.

Never turns off because it's not tied to the senses.

*Matures between the ages of sixteen and nineteen to assume its role. Acts as the guardian, decision maker, and leader. Uses logic to accept or reject information. Connected to the senses and turns off when we sleep.

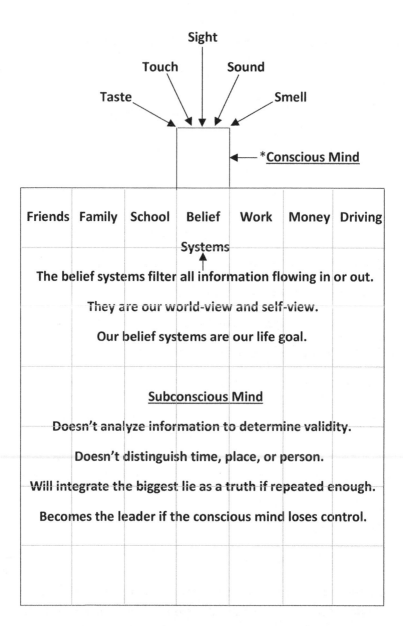

Sight

Touch   Sound

Taste   Smell

*Conscious Mind

Friends	Family	School	Belief	Work	Money	Driving

Systems

The belief systems filter all information flowing in or out.

They are our world-view and self-view.

Our belief systems are our life goal.

Subconscious Mind

Doesn't analyze information to determine validity.

Doesn't distinguish time, place, or person.

Will integrate the biggest lie as a truth if repeated enough.

Becomes the leader if the conscious mind loses control.

*Sense connected, so it can only focus on one thing at a time. Scans thousands of pieces of information each day and can become highly distracted. Determines time, place, and person.

Chapter 2: The Root Cause of Mental Health Disorders

Most people who enter treatment do so because they obviously aren't feeling good. They will talk about having chronic depression, anxiety and mood swings. They will have difficulties with concentration, memory, sleeping, eating, chronic headaches, gastrointestinal problems and other physical discomforts. The mood state is disturbed, distorted and this is impacting their physical health. These are the symptoms they are consciously experiencing. Most people who come into treatment identify that this isn't the first time in their life they have felt this way. When you start examining their history, a picture of repeated cycles of misery appears. As you look at the current stressors in their life, they will point to the relationship, occupational, legal, financial, medical, academic, or substance abuse issues that are triggering their presenting symptoms. Again, when you look back at their history, the same cyclic pattern of such issues is evident.

Most people who enter treatment are consciously aware of the cyclic nature of their difficulties, but don't understand why it happens. When asked how far back they can remember having mood difficulties, they will usually respond by saying in childhood, or adolescence. Treatment should now immediately move in the direction of examining their early childhood experiences. This is the time when their original view of the world was created by family of origin experiences, and early social and academic experiences. From my clinical experience, what is found 99% of the time, when examining this period of a client's life, is a repeated pattern of adverse experiences severe enough to cause their belief systems to form negatively. In some cases, there was one experience severe enough to cause this formation. As they analyze their history, the following belief is what they begin to identify and become consciously aware of. It formed back then, and continues to exist in their mind to the present day:

They believe that bad things are going to continue to happen to them and there is nothing they can do to stop it.

In a nutshell, this is the world-view and self-view born from their early experience that they are still carrying around inside of them. Early on, someone, or something, repeatedly became out of control in their environment which caused them harm. This basic belief is the learning that was created from these adverse experiences and is the underlying cause of almost all mental health disorders. Again, what we believe to be true about the world and ourselves drives our mood structure, perception of reality, our actions, and the eventual outcome of our lives. Happiness and success won't exist as a possibility for a person who carries this around inside of them every day.

The only outcome that will exist is failure and pain, in the form of a lifetime of anxiety and depression.

Bipolar disorder is one of the most commonly known mental health disorders. After treating people with bipolar disorder for almost thirty years, I have come to the conclusion that it is, in most cases, a learned condition. In fact, it is really post-traumatic stress disorder. The exception would be in cases where the mood disorder is substance induced, caused by a traumatic brain injury, or due to some other medical condition. People who suffer from bipolar disorder were exposed to a bipolar environment in early childhood development. The all too familiar scenarios are great disorder in the parental unit. Either one, or both of the parents exposed the child to volatile moods, neglect, abandonment, violence, substance abuse, criminal activities, physical, sexual or mental abuse. The developing child was exposed repeatedly to severe extremes in the environment.

The classic example is of an alcoholic parent who is prone to chronic, volatile, mood and behavioral eruptions. This can come in many other forms, but the bottom line is that the child had repeated reason to be in great fear, or even terror. A child's internal state of mind and mood is completely dependent on the environment, especially early on. A child is dependent on their parents for their sense of well-being, their sense of safety and security. The first and foremost job of any parent is to create a safe and secure home environment. A stable parental structure will produce a stable internal mood structure in the child. Beyond a dirty diaper, being hungry, or a scrape on the knee, a child in a safe environment has no need to be afraid. However, when the parental structure is unstable and prone to abrupt changes of mood and behavior, the child's internal state will grow to exactly mirror that of the world they are being shown. The child learns to live in a constant state of fear.

If this adverse disturbance continues repeatedly in the household environment, the child will never be able to fully relax their psychological, emotional and physical state. This is because the threat of danger continues to exist, causing the child to stay in an anticipatory state of fear and anxiety. They have to stay prepared, on guard, and on high alert for the next bad event to happen. They have to stay in a state of readiness in order to take quick action which in early childhood is usually to run and hide. Because of the constant threat, the child's mood is never allowed to return to a normal and healthy state. The mood structure has now become greatly distorted and this is how a lifelong pattern of repeated struggles with the mood begins. The child's mood is now prone to abrupt, severe mood shifts, completely triggered by the abrupt, severe shifts in their world. The child now walks around daily with a heightened level of chronic anxiety. And, inevitably, when the environment shifts again, the child's mood will jump up quickly to meet the mood of the environment. Depending on the severity of what is happening, the flight or fight response can be triggered in the child's system. This happens when they are so terrified that they truly believe that their life, or someone else's life, is in danger. An Important concept to understand here is that the younger the child, the less it takes to stimulate this response.

In treatment, I have had many people tell me, when reflecting on their parents' verbal fighting in childhood, that they were terrified that their parents would get divorced and their family would be destroyed. A young child will generally have no concept of life without their family together. Their mind is not yet able to conceptualize living without them in the same household. A child, young enough, will believe that if the parents split apart, the family will be destroyed and they will be destroyed, too. Many of these people spoke in terms of fearing death when confronted with the thought of their parents leaving each other, and their world becoming fractured. Because of the repeated threat to their world, and not being able to understand what it really means, chronic parental verbal fighting can be enough to trigger the fight or flight response in a child. If triggered, this means that the child's mood has escalated to the worst state it could ever be in. Repeatedly returning to this fight or flight level causes severe mental, emotional and physical damage over time. Traditionally, it has been thought that only physical violence can trigger this response in the human system. This is not the case at all. Violence does not just describe physical aggression. It also includes the appearance of violence. To a child, a parent losing control verbally, in body language, or in property damage, can be experienced as terror. As mentioned above, parents who routinely verbally fight and yell at each other cause great fear in a child. To review, a child's world, initially, only consists of the environment that the parents create for them. Chronic parental verbal fighting in front of the child is enough to severely threaten that world in the child's eyes. This behavior causes the same extreme internal reaction in a child as their mood jumps up immediately to match the emotional intensity of the parents.

It only takes two extreme incidents for learning to start taking place. This is a very important point, so let me reiterate this point:

It only takes two exposures to extreme events for negative learning to start taking place in a child.

If someone randomly came up behind you during your day and set off an air horn it would cause an instant reaction of severe fear. This experience would cause most people to be driven to the fight or flight level. After it was over, your mood would gradually start to settle and eventually return to its normal state. Because it had only occurred once, the mind would recover pretty quickly, think it was an anomaly, and not expect it to happen again. However, if it happened a second time, you would not be able to fully relax after it was over. You would now be living in a state of fear, anticipating and expecting that it was going to happen again. Your sensory state would become hyper-vigilant, watching and waiting for it to happen again. You would walk through your day constantly on edge – mentally, physically and emotionally. As the days progressed and the air horn continued to go off randomly around you, your previous normal and healthy mood state would be gone, replaced by a chronic state of high anxiety that doesn't go away. And, every time the air horn goes off, your mood would now jump abruptly from this heightened state of new normal to the most severe. In fact, if this situation continued long enough, it wouldn't be long before your mood would start jumping to any sudden change in the environment, and not just the air horn going off. A friend could come up behind you, tap you on the back in order to get your attention and you would react in the same, severe, way. In addition, if you couldn't find a way to stop the air horn from going off, or to avoid its blast, depression would start forming as you became increasingly hopeless that you would ever be able to change the terrible situation you'd now found yourself in. Cycles of depression would also begin appearing because the neurological and physical systems would become exhausted trying to maintain this state of hyper-anxiety, or mania. To conclude, if a person lives long enough in an environment prone to sudden, severe, disturbance, they will quickly develop a mood state that is prone to sudden, severe, disturbance. This is exactly what bipolar disorder is. It's a condition that is primarily learned and developed.

A child chronically exposed to this type of environment becomes overly dependent on their environment for their emotional well-being. What they learn is that if their parental structure is okay, then they are okay. If not, then they aren't. This is what causes a person to be hypersensitive to changes in the environment and the mood to be hyper-reactive to those changes. This is the pattern that is set and will continue to follow the child throughout life unless it is changed. The child learns that change is a bad thing. What they learn is that when the people in their environment get out of control, they get badly hurt. Therefore, change and disorder become synonymous with harm, or bad things happening. Learning is rapidly taking place and the belief systems are being fully shaped by the experiences they are having.

The anticipatory state of fear and anxiety that the child is living in is caused directly by the belief system that is now being integrated into the child's subconscious mind:

Bad things keep happening to me and there is nothing I can do to stop them.

The environment and the people in it are too large and powerful and the child feels tiny and powerless in comparison. Repetition of experience is the key and the subconscious mind will integrate this learning, this belief, as a truth. The conscious mind, not being fully developed yet, can't stop the integration and can't correct the perception of the experience. Long after the child has left the family of origin, they will continue to carry this integrated learning with them into adulthood, unbeknownst to their conscious mind. To review, a belief is an expectation and an expectation becomes a goal.

What becomes integrated in those two belief systems in the subconscious mind becomes our life goal. So, if the above belief system becomes integrated into the subconscious mind, it believes that this is your goal in life and will do everything in its power to fulfill this goal. A terrible goal that states you want continual bad outcome in your life and no way of stopping it. This is what I have found to be the underlying cause, above every other factor, of the repeated cycles of misery and failure that people find themselves in.

Another important concept to understand is that the mood mirrors the thought process. A person walking around daily in an anticipatory state that something bad is going to happen is going to have a mood state that mirrors this. As already pointed out, chronic anxiety is the first mood distortion that appears early on. Depressive states start appearing after the anxiety has formed for two reasons. The first is that a negative belief system doesn't permit the presence of happiness and success in a person's life. The person comes to believe that this type of state doesn't exist for them, maybe for others, but not for them. In fact, they come to believe that they actually don't deserve it. Depressed thinking equals a depressed mood. Depression is driven by the self-view of powerlessness, that nothing they can ever do will change their fortune. This self-view will cause a constant, never ending stream of depression to run through them. The medical term for this state is dysthymia. As this condition continues, unabated, the person will now be prone to developing what are called major depressive episodes. These are characterized by the formation of suicidal ideation, vegetative states in which the person is unable to attend to daily self-care, and sometimes the appearance of psychosis.

These negative belief systems are built initially on fear, though. The fear that something bad is coming causes the person to experience chronic anxiety which is medically termed generalized anxiety. This brings us to the second cause of depressive states. The human central nervous system and brain are not designed to carry the burden of chronic duress for long periods of time before the risk of damage occurs. The human system has an inbuilt response for this. The analogy I use to help people understand this is the circuit breaker in a house. When too much voltage is coming into the electrical system of a house, the circuit breaker trips and shuts it down to save the house from burning down. The same thing happens in the human house. When too much voltage is coming in for too long because the person is in an extended manic state, the system shuts down to save it from damage by going into a more profound depressive state. Manic states are the direct result of an intensification of the belief that something bad is about to happen. The generalized anxiety then escalates into a hyper-state of anxiety driven by the subconscious mind's perception that severe harm is very near. The person becomes stuck in this state until internal damage becomes a reality. This is when their system hits the circuit breaker in order to turn it off which causes the person to be immediately thrown into a major depressive episode. As noted above, these depressive states can become very severe with psychosis, suicidal ideation and vegetative states appearing where the person can't attend to activities of daily living. In these major depressive states, the negative belief systems intensify and the person loses hope that they will ever get better, or ever be happy. The only viable option to resolve the overwhelming problems facing them starts growing in their mind- the thought that they'd be better off dead than to go through the pain anymore. This, then, is how the cycles of manic and depressive states develop in a person who was exposed to repeated extremes in their environment during childhood. They learned to become bipolar because they were exposed to a bipolar environment for too long. People who come into treatment usually believe they are doomed when given a diagnosis of bipolar disorder. There is nothing they can do, they are stigmatized, and all they can do is hope to find a medication that will stabilize them. The knowledge that bipolar disorder is learned gives them hope because anything learned can be unlearned.

As noted earlier, I have come to the conclusion that bipolar disorder is the same as PTSD. PTSD, at its roots, has the same learned belief system due to the exposure to severe traumatic events. PTSD has been most commonly connected to war veterans. What happens to people in active combat situations? Extreme disturbance repeatedly presents in their environment in the form of death and destruction. This is the most severe trauma that a person can experience on the spectrum. Only one such event on this end of the spectrum can cause immediate adverse conditioning. A soldier, who may have had positive belief systems prior to the trauma experience, will now have severely altered negative belief systems about themselves and the world. The world is now a horrible place where horrible things happen and there's nothing that they can do to prevent them. Again, the same basic negative belief system has been integrated into the subconscious mind. Because it's so severe, and accompanied by horrible images and the sensory experience of death and destruction, the conscious mind, even though fully developed, can't stop the process. The experience is usually so swift and severe that it overwhelms the conscious mind's ability to stop the subconscious mind from integrating it as valid. This brings up another situation, other than sleep, when the conscious mind can turn off. Trauma, if severe enough, can cause the conscious mind to turn off because the conscious experience of the event could cause the person to go into shock and die. This survival mechanism is called disassociation. This can happen in adulthood, but is more prevalent in childhood because a child's mind can disassociate easier. Even though the soldier will eventually go home and leave the war environment, the subconscious mind will continue to operate as if the soldier is still in the war zone and is still under the constant threat of death. Consciously, they will understand that they are now a civilian, but the subconscious mind doesn't acknowledge the difference. The veteran, who now has PTSD, will experience the same hyper-vigilance of senses and hyper-reaction of the mood, which is now prone to sudden, severe, shifts when the subconscious mind perceives danger. This state of PTSD will also cause the veteran to experience repeated episodes of severe depression. After almost thirty years of working with mental health disorders, I have come to the realization that most people who enter treatment are suffering from some level of PTSD.

Repeated Extreme Disturbance

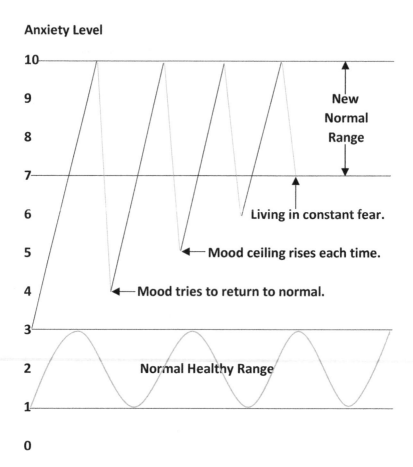

Anxiety Level

New Normal Range

Living in constant fear.

Mood ceiling rises each time.

Mood tries to return to normal.

Normal Healthy Range

The mood continues to be held at the highest level because the extreme disturbance in the environment isn't going away. It's only a matter of time before it happens again.

Integrated Negative Belief System

Anxiety Level

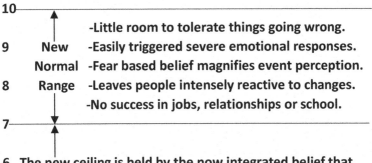

10

               -Little room to tolerate things going wrong.

9   **New**   -Easily triggered severe emotional responses.

       Normal -Fear based belief magnifies event perception.

8   **Range** -Leaves people intensely reactive to changes.

               -No success in jobs, relationships or school.

7

6 The new ceiling is held by the now integrated belief that
something bad is about to happen and it can't be stopped.

5

4

3

2   **Normal Healthy Range**

1

0

Chapter 3: The Awakening and Overcoming Fear

An example of how the subconscious mind now takes over and guides the decision making, based on a belief system of fear, is illustrated in the following actual case:

I had been seeing a veteran in treatment for about a month when he came to a realization during a session. He made a comment, out of the blue, that he didn't own one article of green clothing. This statement was triggered by looking at the green shirt I was wearing that day. This is a very important moment because it is one where the conscious mind is making an observation. These realizations are critical to recovery because the conscious mind needs to start building awareness of what is operating in the subconscious mind so that connections can be made. His subconscious mind, because of the past war trauma, had associated green clothing with death. Literally, his subconscious mind believed that, if he wore green clothing, he or someone else close to him would die, or be severely injured. What is the color of uniform that is most synonymous with a soldier in the military? It is green, of course. Even though he was twenty years removed from the military and combat situations, his subconscious mind continued to operate as if he was still there.

To review, the primary byproduct of trauma is that it leaves, within the person, a great fear that it will happen again. The person will go to great lengths to avoid the trauma again. That is, their subconscious mind will. This veteran's conscious mind knew the difference, knew that it was only a color, that it was only clothing, and that neither had anything to do with death and destruction. However, his conscious mind was overruled by the dominant learning that was stored in his subconscious library. The most critical piece of information to his life had been severely altered to the negative. In the subtle background, whispering in his ear, was the constant belief that the trauma he had experienced before would happen again. Therefore, he needed to be on guard, cautious and extremely careful. If he relaxed for a second, it could mean his death, or the death of someone dear to him. What he talked about in treatment was not really being afraid of his death, but of his loved ones. In the military, he had been a platoon leader and had lost men in battle. He continued to carry tremendous guilt and a feeling of great responsibility for these soldiers' deaths. To him, his family were the soldiers now and he carried even more vigilance to ensure nobody would die under his command again. Even to the point where he would go into the store to buy clothes and purchase anything except clothes that were green. This was not a coincidence, but a pattern, and not a pattern created by conscious choice. It was a completely subconscious choice and his conscious mind didn't know this for twenty years.

So, what is so important about this realization? These are choices being made out of fear. This man continued to live in fear, every hour of every day, that something tragic would befall him. This constant state of fear was affecting his thought process, mood, perception and actions. He was chronically anxious, depressed, and prone to bipolar like mood fluctuations when sensing more severe danger. He misperceived the reality around him and made decisions based on information that applied at one time in his life, but didn't apply at the present time. Because the decisions were based on false information, the choices he made were all wrong. This led to his inability to work, financial ruin, and a broken marriage. The avoidance of green clothing was but the tip of the iceberg and really didn't cause him any trouble in his life. This discovery was only the beginning of waking up to everywhere else his subconscious mind was making decisions to ensure that bad things kept happening in his life. He grew increasingly aware that he was continuing to operate on a premise that was not valid anymore. When the base belief systems are negative, as they were in him, then everything that is created from them is in error and negative. The belief systems we have, which are what we believe to be true, become our expectation for life and our life goal. The subconscious mind will then act on this and do everything it can to achieve this goal unless our conscious mind awakens and becomes aware that the operating belief systems are wrong. Then, and only then, can the conscious mind be engaged to correct them. The next time this veteran came in for his session, guess what color shirt he was wearing?

Green

He had purposely gone out and bought a green shirt with his conscious mind now in full control of the decision making process. He had convinced his subconscious mind that green clothing didn't equal death and to not be afraid anymore. He then wore the shirt to prove to his subconscious mind that his conscious mind was right. This veteran was now freed from one more fear that his subconscious mind had held onto due to the past trauma. One less thing reinforcing that he needed to continue to walk around afraid for his life and afraid for the lives of his loved ones. To continue on the road to recovery, his conscious mind needed to continue its vigilance, discovering more ways that the fear had attached itself to his life and was making decisions that were wrong. In addition, he had to increase his knowledge of how this process was controlling his mood and creating constant states of misery and patterns of failure in his life. With this new knowledge and awareness, his conscious mind was able to continually teach and retrain his subconscious mind to let go of the past and incorporate a new way of thinking. Thinking that was the polar opposite of the negative belief systems he had been carrying around which were born from his past war trauma. The belief that the world was a good place, where good things happened, and he could make them happen. The belief that he had all the talents, skills and abilities in him to be successful and happy. He understood that he was allowing his negative past to continue to dictate who he was as a person- how he thought, felt and acted. He was continuing to live in fear of a part of his life that had been over for twenty years. The above stated positive belief system produces the anticipatory state that everyone needs to have within them. This is the life goal and the life expectation that everyone consciously wants. However, one had better look into the subconscious mind and make sure that this is really what is in there.

Here is another important concept that is absolutely true:

We get what we expect. We get what we anticipate.

However, if the belief system is indeed negative, this is also what happens:

We get what we fear.

Thus far, we have been developing an understanding of what the root cause of any individual's continuous cycles of misery is. In the previous case example, we have begun to address what a person needs to do to recover and to promote wellness. What follows are a couple more case examples to help highlight how healthy recovery is directly connected to the awakening and activation of the conscious mind. Victims of sexual abuse are also victims of trauma, just like the war veteran. Sexual trauma also exists on the most severe side of the trauma spectrum. This case was of a woman who was sexually abused as a child repeatedly between the ages of six to ten years old. During the process of examining her past childhood abuse, she said that every time the perpetrator came into her bedroom to violate her, he would close the drapes across the window. This woman presented to treatment with chronic anxiety, depression and severe mood reactions. She reported that one of her primary stressors was marital discord that had been growing between herself and her husband. She said that one of her husband's chief complaints with her was a pattern of over reacting to what he felt were minor issues. As part of asking her for examples, she disclosed the following situation that had occurred. One day, while sitting in her living room watching television, her husband came into the room. Noticing that there was too much glare coming from the sun through the window, he closed the drapes. Instantly, she became overwhelmed by a severe panic attack. The husband reacted in shock to his wife's extreme response and then moved towards her to try and console her. However, she screamed and desperately tried to get away from him. He was completely taken aback by her actions. Hours later, after her emotional reaction had subsided, she struggled with what had transpired. She, too, didn't know what had happened.

At this point, having reviewed how the mind is structured, it should be clear that it was not her conscious mind that was reacting. In fact, it was her subconscious mind that did. The trauma memories from her past childhood sexual abuse were still active in her mind. Because of the repeated trauma, her belief systems had been distorted, causing her to constantly live in a state of fear that she would get badly hurt again. The images of a man coming into her bedroom as a child and closing the drapes were repeatedly connected to sexual trauma, and the emotional terror that it caused in her. Specifically, her subconscious mind now solely identified a man closing drapes with being sexually abused. To review, the subconscious mind doesn't distinguish person, place or time. As soon as her husband walked into the room and closed the drapes, her subconscious mind read the cue immediately and reacted violently. The subconscious part of her mind actually believed that she was that little girl who was about to be sexually violated again. Her conscious mind was in no way involved in this process. However, once in therapy, she began to make the connections on how her past trauma was continuing to negatively impact her in the present. Awakened with this knowledge, she was able to put her conscious mind in control so that it could now do its job to stop the subconscious mind from allowing her past to continue to dictate her life. She was no longer going to live in fear, and certainly not in fear of her husband closing the drapes again. Her conscious mind was now in position to discover all the ways her subconscious mind was using her past trauma to cause problems in her marital relationship by turning her husband into the monster of her childhood. The problems she had entered treatment with, which had previously been a mystery to her, were now fully understood and viewed as completely fixable.

Social anxiety is a very common treatment issue that people present with. This also, can manifest in varying degrees of severity. Another case example will be used here to show the origins of one particular person's social anxiety. In the fifth grade, this young man had volunteered to do a presentation to his class about the DARE program. This is a program where the school and local police department collaborate to help teach kids about the negative impact of drug use. A police officer was in the classroom on this particular day, along with his teacher. This was his first experience speaking in front of an audience. When it was time for him to do the presentation, his teacher asked him to come up in front of the class. Standing in front of the other students, and with all eyes on him, he now experienced everyone's worst fear when it comes to public speaking. He froze up due to the sudden appearance of terror and could not speak a single word. The teacher, police officer and the class quickly began to realize what had happened. As some of the kids started to laugh, the teacher came to him and tried to calm him down. However, the fear reaction had gone too far and she guided him back to his seat as some of the kids looked at him and snickered. The teacher hushed the kids and completed the presentation with the police officer. He sat there devastated and didn't recover that day. His mother had to be called to come and take him home. What this young man later found out, as he entered treatment at the age of 25, was that he never did recover from it. The experience continued to haunt him long after that fateful day in fifth grade was over.

Based on the event outlined above, and now knowing how the mind works, it should not be surprising to learn what he entered treatment for. He presented with generalized anxiety and panic attacks which were specifically triggered in public situations. If in a one on one situation where someone was trying to communicate with him, he would freeze up and could not speak. He was in the process of developing agoraphobia as he was progressively retreating into his home, which was seen as the only safe place left in the world. Obviously, depression was also present as he had lost hope that he would ever get better, ever live a normal life, or ever be happy. It's important to immediately establish the origins of the presenting symptoms. Sometimes this is not as clear, but if you can find it, it helps greatly in supporting the conscious mind's efforts to teach the subconscious mind the truth. In this young man's case, the origin of his present symptoms was easily discovered.

We quickly came across the fifth grade incident while going through his childhood in the first session. He hadn't thought about it in years, but, as he revisited the memory of it, he immediately saw the parallels between his current symptoms and his early childhood experience. This instant awareness triggered his conscious awakening. He realized that, since that day, he had continued to live in great fear of the experience happening again because his belief systems had been immediately altered. He was carrying around the learning that people are inherently bad and, if given a chance, would hurt him by negatively judging him.

He was holding the belief that performing in front of people in any fashion, even just interacting with a cashier in a store, would cause terrible things to happen. He fully expected that he would fail with regards to anything that had to do with engaging with people, or just being around people. As a result, this young man was unable to work and unable to go to school. The only people in his life he was somewhat comfortable being around were his parents, with whom he lived. As mentioned above, even when he tried to go into a store to buy something, the simple interaction with the cashier would trigger a panic attack.

He realized that continuing to anticipate a repeat of his fifth grade experience was causing him to relive it repeatedly. This concept was highlighted earlier, but it will be good to expand on it here:

We get what we fear because, if the conscious mind isn't awakened, we are destined to relive the fears of our past.

This is what is so important about finding the origin. It gives the conscious mind more ammunition to convince the subconscious mind to let go of the false learning from the origin experience. This young man's conscious mind was the only one that could now look at the origin experience and understand how it was destroying his life. His conscious mind could look at it and see how irrational the conclusion from that experience was. It could question: "Why do I have to continue to be so afraid of people because of something that happened over a decade ago?" That was then, this is now. It should not apply now. It's a different time, place and with completely different people. However, this is what the subconscious mind does when it gets ahold of, and integrates, false learning. It will generalize the learning because it doesn't differentiate time, place or person. It only operates with the basic learning that comes from our experiences. If the conscious mind isn't awake and aware, the subconscious mind will apply the integrated belief system onto everything that looks even remotely similar to the origin experience. In fact, the subconscious mind will be seeking any resource it can use to reproduce it, just like in this young man's experience. However, now armed with this information, he could undergo the process of building his conscious mind's ability to intervene and separate this foundational past experience from completely distorting his current experiences. Slowly, with little steps at a time, he started exposing himself to his fear of people so that he could start learning the truth, that people are good and not to be feared. In addition, to start believing that he was good, worthy and just as good as everyone else. He began to create the understanding that there was never anything wrong with him, but he was made to feel that way because of one bad experience, long ago, in the fifth grade. His conscious mind could now start teaching his subconscious mind that it was done, over with, in the past, and should be of no significance to his life anymore.

It takes a lot of courage to take the necessary steps towards wellness. Especially in the beginning, the subconscious mind doesn't want to let go of what it has believed to be true for so long. It will fight the attempts very strongly because it is being presented with the polar opposite concept of what it believes to be true. The opposite construct being presented to it by the conscious mind will cause an immediate conflict and the subconscious mind will rebel against it, at first. An important concept to understand about the subconscious mind and belief systems is the evolution of increasing intensity the longer it has been integrated. Powerful and false belief systems, such as the ones illustrated in this case example, can end up being viewed by the subconscious mind as critical to the individual's very survival. To review, these belief systems, which comprise the world-view and self-view, are the most important pieces of learning in our mental system. The subconscious mind holds these constructs in importance above all else that is contained within it. What lies in these belief systems becomes our life goal.

The driving goal in this young man's life was to stay away from people because they were viewed as dangerous with the capability of hurting him very badly. Because of the critical nature of the belief systems, they end up becoming connected to the survival mechanism of the human system. Fear and anxiety, if unchecked by the conscious mind, don't stay static in intensity. They will continue to grow and evolve in strength. In this young man's case, his extreme fear of people was created by one experience of being negatively judged. This is what caused his subconscious mind to integrate the belief that people are inherently bad and will hurt him if given the opportunity. Over time, his subconscious mind literally believed that people were to be absolutely avoided because they would cause his actual physical death. As his fear of people intensified, he systematically increased his avoidance of people by going out of the home less and less. Every single time he conceded to his fear of people, he was causing people to become even more dangerous in his mind. If his fears had continued their reign, he would have developed agoraphobia and never left the house. His subconscious mind would have arrived at the belief that if he stepped out of the house, he would be immediately attacked and killed. At this time, I want to highlight the concept being outlined here:

If not stopped, a negative belief system will become so powerful that it will eventually be viewed as necessary to avoid death.

However, this young man had the courage to confront his fears. He also quickly gained an understanding of the concepts presented to him and how to apply them. He learned what he needed to do to change himself and understood why it worked. He got his conscious mind awake, activated and engaged. He immediately went to work on the process of retraining his subconscious mind on what is right and true. He progressively empowered himself and reduced the power of the environment over him. As a direct result of his hard work, this young man, at the end of one year, was able to work full time and attend college. He was finally able to pursue his true life goals which he had not believed possible just twelve months before. He accomplished this by taking small steps in the beginning. Slowly, at first, he built his ability to control his fear reaction around people. He purposely exposed himself to people in ever increasing doses. He would only progress to a more challenging environment when he had learned how to control his fear reactions triggered by the previous environment. All the while, throughout the day, he flooded his subconscious mind with the positive belief system about himself and people that he wanted integrated.

What does it mean by saying that the conscious mind is awake? This means that the conscious mind is now aware and mindful of the false learning that exists in the subconscious mind. It can now become vigilant, watching and waiting for this false learning to show itself. It begins growing an increased understanding of where, when and how the subconscious mind is applying it to present experience. It discerns how this false learning is causing repeated cycles of problems and misery. Once the conscious mind identifies what the root cause is, it can go to work fixing it and correcting it. The case examples that have been outlined so far were reviewed to show this process of conscious awakening as it applied to several individuals' personal experiences. These examples were also given to show that, even though their origin experiences were completely different, the problems manifested in their lives were caused by the same mechanism. Adverse experiences, severe enough, caused false belief systems to be integrated into their subconscious minds and their conscious minds weren't aware of what had happened. Their subconscious minds continued to operate with past learning that didn't apply anymore, causing them to relive the trauma of their past.

Chapter 4: The Failure of Relationships

What the subconscious mind actually believes it's supposed to do is recreate the person's past so it can be relived. This occurs because of two forces which are best illustrated by the following presenting issue that people enter treatment with. A common question I hear in therapy is: "I don't understand it. I keep getting involved with the same type of person and it always goes bad. Why does this keep happening to me?" When things go badly in a foundational relationship with, for example, a parent, the child walks away from it lacking a sense of validation, value, importance, acceptance and feeling that they were loved. This leaves a great hole inside that the child grows up trying desperately to fill through something or someone else. This is the first force that causes recreation of past negative experience. The mind is always trying to resolve problems and this is a critical problem. The subconscious mind will seek to find situations and people as close as possible to the origin experience in order to accomplish this. The mind is driven to finish the origin experience better than how it ended in the past and get what the person missed out on.

We have already covered the second force. These adverse past experiences leave a great fear in the subconscious mind that they will happen again. And, if we are talking about relationships, the fear is created by the view that people are inherently bad and will hurt you if given a chance. As noted previously, this fear becomes an expectation that it will happen again. The expectation creates a constant state of anticipation that the adverse event will occur and that it's inevitable. The subconscious mind now believes this is what you want, that this is your life goal, and will do everything to ensure its successful accomplishment. Can you see the inherent conflict between these two forces? The mind is attempting to achieve what it thinks is a good outcome, but believes it's impossible for it to happen! Additionally, in each of these forces, the subconscious mind is going about trying to accomplish the goal in the wrong way and using the wrong information. Looking at this with our conscious, rational mind, the whole thing is doomed from the start! However, as stated many times at this point, the subconscious mind does not look at things this way. It doesn't distinguish right and wrong, or true and false, and ultimately believes that failure is the goal.

We have already covered how the most fundamental need in childhood is to grow up feeling loved, wanted, valued and accepted by our parents. Through strong parenting, the child will be validated as good and worthy, and grow up with a positive self-view. The child will believe in themselves and be confident. They will believe that they have the right stuff inside of them and have the inherent ability to be successful and happy. Through continued goal setting and accomplishment, this self-view will be increasingly strengthened. This child grows up learning that they have everything inside of them to create situations and experiences that make them feel good. Even when faced with adversity, they believe in their ability to overcome the difficulties and move forward. They look at the people who help them along the way in their journey towards success as adding to them and helping them in their quest. Because this child has developed a healthy view of themselves and the world, they also have a healthy view of people. Because they are already validated inside, they don't need to gain approval or validation from anyone outside of themselves. They don't need it because they already have it. If they get praise or attention from others, it just adds on top of what is already there. They realize that, with or without other people, they can be happy and successful. They don't need someone else to make them feel good, or to feel well. And here, I am specifically referring to close interpersonal relationships and romantic relationships. A child like this won't leave their childhood with a hole to fill and seeking other people to fill it.

When a child grows up rejected by a parent, abused by a parent, and not believing that they're loved by a parent, it leaves a huge hole inside of them. They move forward in life trying to fill it through other people. Their self-view is that they are no good, think that something is wrong with them and don't deserve to be loved. They believe that they aren't worthy in other peoples' eyes. This creates an intense drive state and a desperate need to get what they couldn't get in childhood. This child doesn't believe they have what it takes inside of them to gain the favor or approval of others, but still desperately wants it and seeks it. However, a great mistake is made in attempting to get self-validation through others. It's a critical error to think that, if I can get someone else to accept me, I will be whole, well and happy. This child doesn't know how to do it themselves because they were never taught how. Additionally, they don't understand that, if they don't build it themselves and continue to seek it through other people, they will be doomed to relive the failed origin relationship over and over again. They don't understand that the true basis of well-being is inside of them, not outside, and have to start focusing their efforts on changing their negative belief systems to positive ones. They have to give to themselves what they didn't get in childhood and realize that looking for a surrogate parent to fill the hole will never work.

The primary way anyone achieves happiness is by experiencing that they can accomplish goals through their own self efforts. But before this can even happen, they have to believe that the world is a good place, where good things happen, and they have the ability to make them happen. A child who hasn't been loved believes the opposite and, on top of this, believes that people are bad and will only hurt them, betray them and reject them. This is ultimately the belief that causes people continued cycles of problematic and turbulent relationships that always go bad. This child grows up expecting and anticipating that their close relationships will go the same way as their failed parental relationship. But, at the same time, going into every relationship wanting the other person to accept them, approve of them, and validate them so they can feel good about themselves. As indicated previously, this creates an inherent conflict going into any relationship. On one side, the subconscious mind is afraid of the relationship and is expecting to be hurt by the other person eventually. The subconscious drive, then, is going to be to get away from the person and to end the relationship. On the other side, the person desperately wants it to work out and wants to hold onto the relationship. This desire is also coming from the conscious level of the mind, the logical part of the mind that understands the importance of having good relationships, companionship, and wants to find a partner to move through life with. However, the conscious mind isn't aware of what the subconscious mind is operating with. To review, without the conscious mind being aware, the subconscious drive will dominate the person's thought process, feelings, perceptions and actions. And, here again, I will reiterate a very important concept:

The belief system stored in the subconscious mind is the life goal.

This child's learning early on, what they were taught, was that people will eventually hurt you, betray you and reject you. This is part of their world view. And, because of the powerlessness that a child experiences when faced with chronic mistreatment, their self-view is that there is nothing they can do to stop it. Obviously, this is a terrible life goal for a child to carry into adulthood. This will ensure, if it stays integrated in the subconscious mind, that this child will live a life of constant trouble. The subconscious mind doesn't distinguish right and wrong, or true and false. Whatever it integrates, it automatically believes to be true and also good for you. It believes it's what you want. So, to conclude, this child grows up and enters adolescence and adulthood with a life goal for all close relationships to fail. How does this occur?

The subconscious mind gears the perceptual system to be hyper-vigilant, watching and waiting constantly for this outcome to occur. The senses are wired acutely to identify any cue that can be used as confirmation of its belief. The whole mental system is now in what is called a paranoid state. Even the conscious mind is unknowingly going along now and ignoring the real situation that is going on right in front of its eyes. It's not awake or aware but, in fact, is fast asleep. The perceptual system, because of its hyper-vigilant state, afraid of a bad outcome, is now wired to severely magnify any environmental cue to confirm its belief to be true and to bail out of the relationship. Picture putting a six-foot-high magnifying glass in front of your vision, fixed on the person you're in the relationship with. Every little flaw they have will seem huge and overwhelming. Take the magnifying glass away, and they're barely perceptible. This puts intense pressure on both people in the relationship. For all practical purposes, because of the magnifying glass, the other person in the relationship can't make any mistakes and will have to be just about perfect. This is an impossible expectation to have for anyone. What has been set up now is that any mistake made by the other person will be used as evidence that they are going to hurt them badly, just as their parents did in the past. This mistake, however small it is, will be enlarged to fit the belief. True reality will be distorted to confirm the belief that the other person is just like all people, inherently bad, and with a desire to inflict harm. This process triggers an emotional reaction which is many times greater than what would normally occur if the person was perceiving reality correctly. The emotional reaction will generally mimic the trauma of the origin experience because the subconscious mind actually believes the origin experience is happening again. Remember back to the previous case example of the woman with the sexual abuse trauma and how she reacted to her husband closing the living room drapes. This is exactly what happened to her.

I have found in working with clients, however, that more anger can accompany these reactions in adulthood than was present in the childhood experience. Even as anger and sometimes hate grew in the child towards the parent, especially into adolescence and adulthood when the person certainly now had the ability to unload their anger on the parent, most don't. They hold themselves back for a variety of reasons. However, fast forward to the present with their worst fear confirmed, being hurt yet again by someone who was supposed to love them, and they now have the perfect target in front of them to project their anger onto. What they always wanted to say or do to their parent, but couldn't, can now be unleashed. Not everyone reacts this way, but the overall point is that whatever the emotional reaction triggered, it will be way beyond what the actual situation calls for. How is the other person in the relationship going to react now? They're now hurt, confused and their attitude towards their partner changes negatively. Can you see where this is headed? If unchecked by the conscious mind, this process will continue and the person will end up getting exactly what they expected which is the destruction of the relationship. Not because the other person rejected them, but because they pushed them away. They rejected them first. All because the subconscious mind was allowed to continue to direct decision making based on the false learning created by bad experiences with other people in their past. The person in the current relationship had nothing to do with this. However, they mistakenly believed that they were one and the same, unable to distinguish the difference. And, of course, this is the way the subconscious mind will make sure the person continually relives bad relationships from the past. It is important to repeat this point:

We get what we expect.

The subconscious mind will actively seek situations and people that resemble, as closely as possible, the failed relationship of origin. If it's a parent, then the subconscious mind will search, based on the known profile of the parent, for an individual that is the closest match. Again, this is solely a subconscious process and the conscious mind isn't involved at all. The subconscious mind is looking to relive the past, so it needs to find a surrogate for the relationship of origin, the individual who mistreated the person and caused the negative belief systems to form. Because it lacks the ability to use logic, the subconscious mind believes this is what you want and that it's good for you.

Another case example will help to illustrate how this process plays out in a person's life. How the subconscious mind operates to ensure continued relationship failure by selecting a person to get involved with who is the same profile as the relationship of origin. As outlined previously, there are two forces that drive reliving adverse past experiences. The first is the great fear that they will happen again, and the second is that our mind is always looking to resolve unfinished business from the past. Relationships of origin that went bad are unresolved problems that the mind will continue to look to resolve and end better. However, unless the conscious mind knows that the wrong belief about people is being used by the subconscious mind, this is destined to always end the same way as it originally did. In order to change the outcome, the person has to integrate the healthy view of people and themselves.

A good analogy I like to use is of an ice cream sundae with your favorite ice cream. It's really good with all the toppings, the extras on it, the chocolate syrup, whipped cream and the cherry on top. But, even without the toppings, just with the ice cream standing on its own, it tastes great. We are the ice cream and we are completely fine and good with or without the toppings which represent, for our discussion here, close interpersonal relationships, especially romantic ones. When a person has integrated this belief into their subconscious mind, then they will attract and be attracted to healthy individuals. When the opposite belief system is in place, that people are inherently bad and will eventually burn you, then people who can fulfil this role will be chosen. This person believes that good people really don't exist and, even if they did, they don't deserve them anyway because they are bad themselves. The subconscious mind will then reject the good people that are out there and, instead, focus on selecting people with the same belief systems. There is absolute truth to the saying, like minds attract like minds. But again, this is no coincidence. Rather, it's a choice, but a choice controlled by the subconscious level of the mind. The conscious mind isn't aware of what's happening. "Why do I keep ending up with the same person over and over again?" This question, frequently asked by clients in therapy, is actually coming from their conscious mind.

A man came into treatment with this very question. He was, at the time, around 45 years old. He had one failed marriage when he was in his early twenties and multiple failed relationships afterwards. He had grown completely frustrated with this pattern in his life and tired of the resulting depression and anxiety. The growing belief in him was that he would never find anyone to spend the rest of his life with and would eventually die alone. It was easy to see the negative belief system operating within him. Immediately, we got to work on his family of origin experiences. His father was an intrastate trucker and was gone for long periods of time away from the family. My client was the youngest child and only boy. He had three older sisters. His father was described as a good man who treated him well when he was home. He described his mother very differently. She had a problem with alcohol and was prone to sudden mood shifts which were volatile in nature. The mother would get violent at times when in these moods. He realized that she shouldered the burden of running the household and raising four children. He recognized the stress she was under. As he reflected on his memories, he remembered that his mother was very critical of him and he could do nothing right in her eyes. She singled him out for physical punishment, but didn't discipline his sisters this way. He remembered that there was a great difference in treatment between him and his sisters. This disparity in treatment caused him to resent his sisters. It made him feel that he was different, and that there was something wrong with him. During the times when his father was home, the home environment was often disturbed by intense verbal fighting between the parents. As my client talked about his childhood experiences, he became emotional and tears welled up in his eyes. This is a very common reaction when people are asked to tell the story of their early childhood experiences. The intense emotional reaction is evidence of how much unfinished business is connected to these experiences, and how much impact they are still having in their lives.

These were the critical early experiences that shaped his view of people, women in particular, his view of marriage, and his view of himself that he was still walking around with. As a child, he was powerless to affect a positive change in his world. He didn't have the skills or abilities to resolve the problems that were occurring in his life and no help came to stop what was happening. Having already outlined the forces and mechanisms that cause people to repeat and relive past bad relationships, how was his mother going to impact his future female relationships? Having uncovered his childhood past, we got to work looking at all his failed romantic female relationships, starting with his early marriage. We began creating a profile of all of these women, the purpose being to identify the pattern so that his conscious mind could finally see it. It didn't take long for him to see that all but one of the women had the same core personality traits as his mother did. Let me repeat this:

All of the women were the same as his mother, except for one.

When this conscious realization hit, and he connected the parallels between his mother and his history of failed romantic relationships, he again released a lot of powerful emotion. This is a very sobering moment for people in treatment. When laid out for the conscious mind to examine, the reason for their continuous cycles of problem relationships becomes readily apparent. I explain, at this time in treatment, that this process isn't designed to further intensify their anger towards the parent of origin. Rather, it's to remove the mystery from a phenomenon in their life that had been previously unexplainable. As mentioned before, this helps the correction process that the conscious mind now has to undertake to end the cycles of misery. Critical to my client's recovery process was a conscious understanding of the profile of women his subconscious mind would select for him. This profile was being sought because his subconscious mind believed that this was the type of women he wanted and that this type of woman would be good for him. Obviously, in reality, it was the exact opposite that was true. He needed to become consciously aware of this wrong profile so that his conscious mind could actively stop him from continuing to get involved with this type of women. He could no longer allow his subconscious mind to make this choice because it was costing him his life. However, now armed with the necessary information and awareness, his conscious mind would now make the choice.

What about the one woman who didn't fit his mother's profile? There was a time in his life when his job took him to Germany. While living in Germany, he fell in love with a young woman. After only several months together, he realized there was something different about her. He actually proposed to her and they were to be married. But, as the wedding day drew closer, he started getting increasingly uncomfortable with the idea of being married to her. He found that he started to find flaws with her and used these as reasons why he shouldn't marry her. This discontent continued to grow until he called off the wedding. As he talked about this woman in session, a different type of emotion came from him. There was a sadness connected to her, and this time in his life, because he had always felt that he made a mistake. However, he didn't know why he felt this way. After developing her personality profile, and then comparing it with the profile of the other women, it became obvious why. She was the exact opposite. She was stable of mood, kind to him, creative, her actions lined up with her words, she was financially stable, she had a good job, took responsibility when she was wrong, she didn't take out her problems on him, and she didn't have a substance abuse problem.

Why had he rejected her? She was the right one and he had rejected her because of all her good qualities. He came to realize that it was her good characteristics that he started finding flaws with and his subconscious mind had turned them into negatives. Looking back, he identified that what had primarily happened was that he had started to increasingly believe that she was too boring for him and wasn't exciting enough. In contrast, he remembered viewing the other women, who were all wrong for him, as exciting and stimulating to be around. His subconscious mind had turned all their negative, volatile, and troublesome qualities into positives. In his mind, fighting, arguing, constant turmoil and trouble had become good times. This, again, was a very powerful and sobering moment for him. However, very important to him in terms of his personal growth so that he would never make the same mistake again. When he put the two contrasting profiles side by side so his conscious mind could analyze them, he saw the truth immediately. Now, with his conscious mind awake, aware, and armed with the right information, he could make the self-correction. He was able to realize that his subconscious mind was operating with completely wrong information and that this was why his relationships went so badly. And, when the truly right woman came along, his subconscious mind rejected her because it believed she was all wrong for him. To review, because the subconscious mind doesn't distinguish between right and wrong, right and wrong can get completely turned around within a person. His subconscious mind, without his conscious mind knowing, was continuing to reproduce his failed relationship with his mother over and over again in his life.

Unfortunately, there was no fairy tale ending to this story. He didn't reconnect with the woman he met and almost married all those years ago in Germany. However, there was still a very good ending for him. He realized that he wasn't doomed to repeat the mistakes of the past. He developed the ever growing confidence and hope that he could find her again, in the form of another woman. His conscious mind now knew which women to avoid and what type of woman to seek. Additionally, his conscious mind was in a position to block all attempts by the subconscious mind to sabotage his efforts to build a relationship with the right woman. Whenever he started feeling discomfort with such a woman, or found himself starting to find flaws, he would understand immediately where this was coming from and stop it. His conscious mind would then be able to reaffirm the true and correct perception of the relationship, thereby maintaining conscious control.

The constant vigilance over this process, and repetitive self-correction, would eventually lead to his subconscious mind falling in line with the conscious mind, both united with the right information. Overtime, his subconscious mind would stray to the negative belief systems less and less. It would inevitably drop the old, wrong view of women and replace it with the new, right version. His conscious mind was now doing its job, teaching and guiding his subconscious mind towards the truth. He came to understand that there was never anything wrong with him, but, instead, he had been made to feel bad about himself and other people because of someone else in his early life who had been very ill. The problem was never him but, rather, it was that he had continued to carry forward his unresolved family issues in the form of false belief systems about himself and women. Now that his conscious mind had become awakened and activated, he realized that he could choose to have happy and successful relationships. He awakened to the truth that the quality of a person's life and relationships is a direct reflection of the quality of what they choose to believe to be true about themselves and the world.

Chapter 5: The Psychology of Dependency and the Psychology of Happiness

I consider substance abuse to be a mental health issue. They are one in the same to me. In all my years of working with people who come to treatment with substance abuse issues, I have concluded that substance abuse is a symptom of an underlying mood disorder. And, because the mood directly mirrors the thought process, the underlying cause of substance abuse is the same basic negative belief system that is at the root of almost all mental health issues. This has already been outlined but bears repeating again. I can't emphasize enough that this is what has to be changed for people to get better:

Carrying around the constant belief that bad things are going to continue to happen and there's nothing that can be done to stop it.

The area of substance abuse leads to a very interesting concept. The concept that a person's thought process can actually affect the receptors and neurotransmitter system that exists in the brain. I refer to this system as the reward circuitry. This neurological system is responsible for healthy mood regulation by promoting and facilitating positive mood states and resisting negative mood states.

The depiction of this system can get complicated so, over the years, I have stripped it down to what I believe are the basic essentials. This is so people in treatment can grasp the process quickly and see how substance abuse damages this part of the brain and how the process of physiological addiction unfolds.

The process of tolerance to a substance occurs when the body compensates and tries to restore balance to this neurological system. The bottom line is that the chronic use of drugs, including alcohol, will cause the body to systematically shut down the receptors and the uptake of the neurotransmitters. The two most commonly known neurotransmitters are dopamine and serotonin, but there are many others. The user then compensates by using more of the drug in order to get the same high. The body and user then go through this back and forth adjustment as the addiction process unfolds, getting increasingly worse. This describes the process of physiological addiction.

Eventually, the user can't sustain positive mood states without the drug being in the brain. This is because the body has shut down the brain structure that is normally and naturally responsible for healthy mood states. Drugs have a short life in the brain and when they are gone there is nothing to support the mood of the user. With the drug gone from the brain, the mood of the user starts crashing without the proper functioning of the neurotransmitters. This crash is felt in the form of deepening depression, anxiety, agitation and anger. The mood becomes unstable and the user has to get the drug back into the brain as quickly as possible to bring the mood back up. This crash is also accompanied by a variety of physical withdrawal symptoms, depending on the drug consumed, but I'm only going to focus on the mood reaction that occurs. If the user doesn't get help and enter into substance recovery, the escalating use of the drug will eventually lead to permanent damage of the reward circuitry. The individual will now be facing serious psychiatric issues due to the brain damage incurred.

Substance induced schizophrenia and severe mood disorders will now plague them with increasing intensity. At this point, the substance user usually starts having repeated inpatient psychiatric hospitalizations and will be placed on psychiatric medications in an attempt to stabilize their condition. However, as soon as they are discharged, they will start using drugs again and abandon their psychiatric treatment. If unabated, the process will continue and the brain, along with the mental and emotional condition, will deteriorate further during this phase with depression becoming a growing threat. At this point, the substance user is at high risk for suicide and a great number of impulsive suicide attempts occur here. This is because the only solution to their growing problems appears in the form of suicide. Sadly, far too many people on this path complete suicide when it could have been prevented.

I've just outlined the physiological process of addiction. I will now address the psychological side. After years of treating people suffering from substance abuse, I have found that they all had a chronic mood disorder pre-dating their substance abuse. This observation comes from my own clinical background and experience. Because the mood directly follows the thought process, this means that they had negatively altered belief systems before they ever touched drugs. When the substance abuse issue is looked at this way, it becomes clear that substance abuse is yet another symptom of the individual carrying around belief systems that have gone negative. Whenever I treat anyone in treatment, I always immediately go back and try to find their origin experiences and substance abuse is no different. To review, origin experiences are the ones that caused the belief systems to negatively distort. With substance abuse, I almost always find the same pattern of early adverse experiences, especially in the family of origin. As noted previously, these adverse experiences can also occur in other environments, not just the family of origin. However, in my clinical experience, they overwhelmingly occur in the family of origin.

Before a person with substance abuse issues even has their first experience with drugs, their belief systems have been turned completely negative. They have been walking around in a state of anticipation that bad things will continue to happen to them and there is nothing they can do to stop them. How does this state set a person up for substance abuse and addiction? It sets them up for substance abuse because what we believe to be true drives our mood state. Any person walking around with negative beliefs about themselves and the world inevitably develops chronic anxiety and depression. There is no room for happiness in this type of belief system. Happiness doesn't exist for them and there are no opportunities to change this. To a young person with this condition, home is a downer, school is a downer and the only brief glimpses of happiness they get are the moments they get with their friends. Unfortunately, for some pre-teens and teens, this isn't even possible because of toxic social environments and bullying. However, young people with negative belief systems find themselves gravitating towards other young people with like minds. If the child hasn't had their first experience with drugs in the home, then they will have their first opportunity with their peers. I would like to clarify at this point that whenever the term, drugs, is referenced, this includes alcohol. Drugs and alcohol will generally start appearing around them in their pre-teen to early adolescent years.

What will the first experience of drugs be like for a young person walking around with chronic anxiety and depression? The interesting concept I alluded to at the beginning of this particular discussion is that our belief systems directly impact the reward circuitry in the brain. Our thoughts directly impact our bodily system and the brain is part of this system. Because our integrated belief systems become our life goal, the mental and bodily systems will use every resource external and internal to achieve the believed goal.

To review, whatever has been integrated into the subconscious mind has been validated as true. When a person believes that only bad things will come to them and they are powerless to affect a positive change, this is a command to the body to suppress the reward circuitry. The very system in the body that is responsible for the experience of happiness, joy and pleasure. However, happiness and joy have no place in such a belief system. The person believes that happiness doesn't exist for them, maybe for others, but not for them. In addition, they usually have never been taught how to stimulate this neurological system naturally. They haven't been given the opportunity to learn positive coping skills and how to internally regulate their own thoughts and mood. The person hasn't gone through the process of discovering, and repeatedly using, productive activities and goal accomplishment to stimulate this part of the brain and feel good.

An individual who has a positive belief system has learned how to do these things and continues to strengthen their ability and skills in this area. This is due to their belief that good things happen in this world, they are supposed to happen to them, and they can make them happen. A young person with this type of positive belief system has been taught how to correctly utilize this part of the brain. As a result, their body reinforces this crucial neurological system, making it stronger and more efficient. The body will actually add receptors and increase production of the neurotransmitters. This is true with any part of the body and the brain is no exception. If you've ever had a broken arm or leg and had that body part in a cast, what does it look like when the cast is finally taken off? Due to lack of use, it has atrophied and is small and weak compared to the other limb. When you start exercising and using it again, it will eventually return to the same size and strength of the other side. If you've ever trained athletically or exercised strenuously, you know that the body compensates by making the whole system stronger and with a much improved mind-muscle connection. The old saying, use it or lose it, is very true. More accurately, though, it should look like this when talking about the brain:

Use it correctly or lose it.

Unfortunately, a child who has grown up with false belief systems has an atrophied reward circuitry due to lack of proper use. Returning to the question above, what happens when this young person now consumes their first drug? What do you think the reaction will be? The effect of the drug will be many times more powerful than it would be in a young person with a fully operating receptor and neurotransmitter system. I will argue here that a young person with a powerfully built positive belief system will not even try drugs. But, for the sake of our discussion here, I am including this for comparison. Why is the effect of drugs so magnified in a child with negative belief systems? Because this child doesn't believe they can do anything to affect positive change in their life. They don't know how to independently manufacture happiness and pleasure and, in fact, don't believe happiness exists for them in this world. This child has been walking around in a chronically anxious and depressed state that has become normalized. They haven't been able to find anything in their life that has made them feel really good. I have found that most young people who come into treatment in this condition describe themselves as being numb, or neutral. This is their normal, walking around state and the only change that occurs to it is when they are angry or very depressed.

As soon as the intoxication and high of the drug kicks in, this all changes for them. Suddenly, the realization hits that they have found it! What has happened correspondingly on the physiological side in the brain is that previously suppressed neurotransmitters have been released in the form of a huge burst. This is why the chemical experience of the drug in this young person is many times more powerful than in a child with properly functioning neurotransmitters. Sadly, for most young people in this mental and emotional state, it's the first time in their life they have felt good, this good. It's the first time that they have gone from numb to a positive mood state. However, they don't realize that it's only a deception and a counterfeit experience of happiness and pleasure. But, because their subconscious mind is looking for anything that will assist towards accomplishing the goal of continued bad outcome and subsequent misery, they don't understand that they've just been hijacked and are about to complicate their lives in ways they never could've imagined. The subconscious mind, with repeated substance use, will wrap around the belief that the drug enhances the quality of their life and makes them a better person. This is the great danger and the siren's song of any drug. Because the belief systems were already negative prior to first use, this child is now completely set up to fall for this lie. This is how the psychological process of addiction commences.

As the physiological addiction grows and the body and brain increasingly can't function without the drug, the psychological component grows in the same direction. The belief that the quality of life is enhanced by the drug intensifies with continued substance use. It doesn't stay static. It has been previously discussed that any negative belief system, if not stopped, will undergo three stages of intensification and ultimately become connected with death. The drug use is working towards becoming enmeshed with the survival mechanism of the human system. The belief steadily marches forward, growing stronger with every use, until the subconscious mind, in the end stages of addiction, fully believes that the person will die if they stop using. It evolves from the initial belief that the drug enhances the quality of life, moving next to the drug being viewed as critical for the continuation of life and then finally to the belief that life will end without it. This is why the defense mechanisms, known as denial, are so strong in addiction and a person will continue to use drugs even though it is actually killing them.

The continued escalating use of the drug will eventually take up the whole top level of the subconscious mind. This top row of compartments is reserved for the most important and vital information and priorities in a person's life. The things we should be spending most of our time and energy on. Things like family, good friends, work, finances, hobbies, school, religion, positive recreation, goals and the steps being taken towards advancing positive growth. As the drug increasingly consumes the person, it will take up more and more space in the top level. This means that the real priorities will start being pushed out and down the hierarchy of the subconscious mind as they are neglected. When this process occurs, the user will begin experiencing serious consequences in their life. The person's good relationships, work and financial status will start to suffer. This is the time when legal issues can surface such as possession, theft, and DUI convictions. As the addiction process continues to unfold, serious health issues can also start appearing. However, despite the mounting evidence to the contrary, the subconscious mind clings to the belief that the drug enhances the quality of the person's life. It's necessary and critical to keep on using and, as noted previously, the subconscious mind will eventually come to believe that death will accompany cessation of the drug. Obviously, when examined by the conscious mind, the exact opposite is true. The continued use of the drug is actually destroying the individual's life. The real truth is that, if they keep on using, they will die.

The process of growing substance abuse is one of the best ways to illustrate how powerful the subconscious mind can be when not under the control of the conscious mind. It demonstrates how right and wrong and true and false can become completely twisted around in the wrong direction. Drug addiction also shows how devastating the effects are on the person's life when the subconscious mind is operating with wrong information. The subconscious mind will use every lie, manipulation, rationalization and resource that it can to keep the drug use going. Powerful defense mechanisms are built around the drug like a fortress to defend against anyone or anything that will try to stop the use. Family members and close friends will make the attempt, but their efforts will be met with strong resistance. As referred to earlier, this is what is known as denial. No one else outside of the user can crack that fortress of denial. The only thing that can fracture it is the person hitting rock bottom. Hitting rock bottom is a phrase commonly used to describe when a person with addiction starts accumulating enough serious consequences to wake up their conscious mind. Something happens of such a severe nature that they can't deny the problem anymore, as much as they try. Rock bottom is different for everyone. For some, it takes less than others. Sadly, some people who are addicted never hit rock bottom. They continue to use the drug even as their lives crumble around them and their bodily organs begin to fail. In the end, tragically, they will die.

The way to successful, sustained recovery for a person with substance abuse issues is the same as for a person coming into treatment with mental health issues. If the negative, false belief systems driving the substance abuse aren't changed, the individual won't recover. Once aware of the problem, the conscious mind has to convince the subconscious mind to let go of the false belief systems and replace them with the positive antithesis. The person has to learn now what wasn't learned early on:

The world is a good place where good things happen and I can make them happen.

And more specifically, drugs have no place in the above life goal.

They have to start building the internal ability to regulate the thought process and mood by gaining greater and greater conscious control. Very important in the process of substance abuse recovery is re-awakening the suppressed reward circuitry. The individual now has to explore and engage in natural methods to repeatedly stimulate it. The body has to be made to realize that the person wants to use it so that it will turn on long turned off receptors and start producing and releasing the neurotransmitters again. This process takes time and the former user is vulnerable to relapse during this period because the mood can be very problematic. They rightfully removed and stopped using the only coping tool that had been developed to self-medicate chronic anxiety and depression. Whenever even a negative coping mechanism is removed, it must be replaced with numerous productive and positive ones. If the reward circuitry is constantly stimulated the right way, it will re-awaken. But remember, it will only ultimately re-awaken if the positive belief system that supports happiness as a reality is integrated into the subconscious mind under conscious direction.

There is an old Native American story that very simply summarizes how the mind works. The story is of a Native American elder talking to his son. He tells his son that in every person's mind there is a battle between two wolves. The one wolf is hateful, weak, angry, deceitful and jealous, full of all the negative characteristics. The other wolf is loving, kind, strong, honorable and trustworthy, full of all the good characteristics. After the father is done describing the two wolves, the son looks at his father and asks, "Father, which one wins?" The father looks deeply into his son's eyes and responds, "The one you feed."

The person's job in recovery is to now starve the negative addiction thinking and actions, and feed the thoughts and actions that support abstinence. The individual needs to engage in substance abuse treatment to reinforce this process. This can consist of detox, inpatient or outpatient substance abuse treatment and consistent Alcoholics Anonymous or Narcotics Anonymous meeting attendance.

In addition, the person needs to spend increasing time and energy on the right priorities such as family, positive friends, exercise, productive relaxation, religion, music, art, job, education and goal accomplishment. Repeated focus on these areas will establish them back into their rightful place in the subconscious hierarchy which is in the very top row. All the while, the recovering person needs to consciously reinforce the positive belief of the self and the world that has to be either re-established or established for the first time in the subconscious mind. It's very important to extinguish the deceptive thinking that supported the drug use everywhere they recognize it occurring. A lie started the use and increasing lies and deception supported continued use. This growing dishonesty begins to infect increasing areas of the person's life and ends up becoming the way they live. Lying, cheating and stealing are the negative patterns of thinking applied everywhere.

Even if a person has established early recovery and has stopped drugging, but continues to use manipulation and deception in other areas of their life, they are on the sure road to relapse on the drug. Why is this? Because they are feeding the very core of the substance abuse problem they had. The substance abuse is conditioned and directly chained to the pattern of dishonesty. If fed enough, it will cause the now dormant substance abuse compartment to be pulled back up through the levels of the subconscious mind again. Whether one is in recovery for mental health or substance abuse issues, right thinking and action has to be practiced in every aspect of life. If not, the door will be opened for these negative belief systems, and all the misery they bring with them, to be re-integrated back into one's life. The conscious mind must remain vigilant at all times to reject any and all negative thoughts. On the other side, it must maintain constant focus on accepting and cultivating positive, constructive thoughts and experiences. Insuring that the conscious mind remains awake and doing its job is the only way to create true mental and emotional well-being.

Another case example will be used here to illustrate the above points about the importance of extinguishing the core negative thinking that created and supported the drug addiction everywhere in one's life. This case will show how feeding this thinking will lead to the drug addiction gaining expression through other forms until it finally establishes itself out in the open again. The first is of a client who came in after inpatient detox and treatment for crack cocaine addiction. This was his fifth attempt at recovery. He reported that he would always start off strong in his recovery, but would inevitably fall back into use of the drug. He was losing hope that he would ever be able to overcome his addiction. This man was in his early fifties and had already experienced severe legal, financial and occupational consequences due to his drug addiction. He came into treatment with yet another legal charge of drug possession and now his marriage of 22 years was at great risk. I made sure he was participating in our intensive outpatient substance abuse program and was attending frequent Narcotics Anonymous meetings, and then got to work on his subconscious mind.

We quickly found negative patterns that were evident in all of his past attempts at sustained abstinence. One pattern was present whether he was using crack or not. The other only surfaced when he wasn't using the drug. The first was a pornography addiction and the second was shoplifting. When not using, he would go into Home Depot or Lowes and steal a screw or a bolt, something very small and not worth much money at all. Because he was in the construction business, he was frequently in these stores and always had to walk out with something that he stole. In his past treatment episodes, he never identified that this compulsive action was connected to his drug use. We worked on raising his awareness that they were directly linked and that he had to address this behavior, and the thinking that drove it, or he would be on his way to relapse on the drug again.

This man realized that the core deceptive thinking underneath his drug use was also at work when he shoplifted. He got in tune with what was happening internally when he committed this act and how it mimicked his crack cocaine use. He talked about the stimulation of it, how his excitement levels would rise on his way to the store and how this state would increase in intensity as he got ever closer to the act. He realized how this was exactly the same internal process that would occur as he got closer to the drug house to score his crack cocaine fix. The excitement level of the act of theft would escalate in direct proportion to the fear of being caught as he walked towards the store exit and left the building. The emotional rush of this whole experience was what he was seeking, and, while not nearly as powerful as crack cocaine, it accomplished the job of getting high for the time being.

With his new knowledge and awareness, he understood that he had to view his acts of shoplifting as the same as relapsing on crack. If he walked out of a store with a stolen item, then he had just relapsed on crack cocaine. He had to understand that the subconscious mind was using shoplifting as a stepping stone to get back to what it really sought which was crack cocaine. The shoplifting would only serve as a surrogate for so long because the high produced wasn't nearly as satisfying as the high that crack cocaine gave him. He realized that if he didn't get to work with his conscious mind to extinguish the shoplifting, he would never kick his crack cocaine addiction for good. When we examined the function of pornography in his life, he came to understand that it served the same purpose as the shoplifting and the drug. If he didn't stop his pornography addiction, he would never be able to end his crack cocaine addiction. He now viewed them as one and the same because he now realized that the shoplifting, pornography and crack cocaine use were just outward expressions of the real core problem which was the negative lie, cheat and steal thinking that he continued to utilize in his life. Of course, he also came to understand that this thinking was a direct extension of the negative belief systems that had been integrated into his mind about himself and the world that he had been carrying around for decades. These negative belief systems were continuing to manifest in his life, creating a never ending cycle of problems that he had to deal with. The shoplifting, pornography, and, especially, the crack cocaine use were perfect vehicles to accomplish the goal his subconscious mind believed he wanted. To review, the negative goal is always the same and it was no different in him. This goal being:

Trouble will continue to happen in my life and there's nothing I can do to stop it.

He fully realized that if he didn't change this belief system, he would continue to experience unending cycles of misery and never successfully achieve abstinence from crack cocaine. As a result of this new awareness, he was able to focus on the real origin of his addiction and start addressing the two other connected forms of it which were the shoplifting and pornography. By changing his old, negative belief system to a positive one, and extinguishing the shoplifting and pornography use, he was able to achieve his long time goal of full, sustained remission from crack cocaine.

Here is another example of how in depth a person in mental health or substance abuse recovery has to go with their thinking in order to sustain their recovery. I had been working with another client who was in sustained remission of drug addiction for six years. He was very established in his Narcotics Anonymous program, but had presented to treatment for severe depression and anxiety which was causing him to shut down in most other areas of his life. He had been increasingly letting go of all of his daily responsibilities and was starting to have suicidal thoughts. He was unable to work and had gained 150 pounds because he had replaced the drug with over eating food to self-medicate his mood disturbance. As a result, serious health issues were beginning to appear that were threatening his life. Despite gaining initial success in stopping his drug use, he was unaware that the drug use was only a symptom of a much deeper problem. This problem still existed and, even though he had removed the primary method of creating trouble in his life, his subconscious mind was continuing to look for other ways to continue achieving the goal of repeated misery. He was proud of his accomplishment of bringing his drug addiction into remission, but it wasn't good enough as he still couldn't find happiness in his life. Through proper treatment, this client discovered that his belief systems had gone negative early on in childhood due to severe family dysfunction and being exposed to the chronic volatility of his mother who had never been treated for bipolar disorder. From the beginning, he had learned to expect repeated bad outcome in his world. He was able to identify that this negative expectation and goal for his life was continuing to drive his current problems and unhappiness. He understood that stopping his drug addiction wasn't enough and, if he didn't alter his long held belief about his future outcome, he would never find the happiness he sought. He woke his conscious mind up to the root cause of his current problems and started working hard to change what his subconscious mind believed to be true. His conscious mind became vigilant and the positive changes he sought started to unfold around him.

This man lost weight, returned to work and became activated in all the areas of his life that had been previously shut down. As a result, the quality of his mood improved as the quality of his thought process improved. The suicidal ideation disappeared as he had a renewed confidence and hope for the future outcome of his life. Additionally, he had identified several other negative compulsions that he had subconsciously replaced his drug addiction with. It has already been mentioned that over eating was used as a surrogate, but he also realized that he had a sex addiction in the form of frequenting strip clubs and using prostitutes for sex. He came to understand that his continued abstinence from drug use was at great risk and would eventually fall if he kept feeding these other addictions. The fact that he had made it six years without relapse on the drug was remarkable, but the tell-tale signs that it was just around the corner were there. As his depression had deepened, he recalled how the thought of using was on the rise and that it had even started invading his nightly dreams. He realized that not only was he fast approaching drug use again, but, because of the severe depression and suicidal ideation, he had actually been heading towards a suicide by overdose.

A year later in treatment, he was growing in success and happiness, and the path he was on before he entered treatment was a distant memory. His continued success was the direct result of maintaining his conscious mind in a state of vigilance to block the negative mind and promote the positive mind. He was constantly on guard, watching his thinking and actions. The following situation he brought into a session is a great example of how in depth this mental process needs to go in order to achieve success. One day, this man came into session and recounted the following scenario that had occurred a few weeks earlier. At that time in his treatment, he was on a maintenance phase of treatment and would schedule a session only on an as needed basis. He was at the gym where he exercised and was finishing up in the locker room, getting ready to leave, when he noticed a pair of sunglasses laying on a bench. He looked around and there was no one else in the locker room. His first thought, which was the right one, was to turn them into the front desk so the person who left them would be able to get them back. However, the more he looked at the sunglasses, another thought started to appear. He tried on the sunglasses and discovered that they were a good fit and looked really good on him. He looked at them closer and saw that they were a very good brand and probably pretty expensive. It's very apparent what was taking place in his mind at this point. His negative mind was coming out and trying to talk him into doing the wrong thing. He was actively engaged in the battle of the two minds, but in this situation the negative wolf temporarily gained the upper hand and he walked out of the gym with the sunglasses. However, because of all the hard work he had done in strengthening the positive wolf, the battle wasn't over.

As he drove towards his Narcotics Anonymous meeting, which is where he was headed after the gym, he began to experience increasing guilt over what he had done. He couldn't believe that he had just allowed himself to make a choice to steal a pair of sunglasses from someone else. In addition, because of his newly gained knowledge and awareness that this act was the same as relapsing on his old drug, he knew what he had to do even before he got to the meeting. He used his Narcotics Anonymous meeting as a place to talk about what he had done and to reinforce that, if he allowed himself to get away with this, he was one step closer to relapsing on the drug. After the meeting was over, he drove right back to the gym and turned the sun glasses in to the person at the front desk. As he recounted the end of his experience, he talked about how good it made him feel to know that he had done the right thing. In addition, he knew that, because he had waged the battle and his positive mind had ultimately won in the end, he had grown even better and stronger as a person. This is how vigilant the conscious mind needs to be in order to create opportunities for success.

At this time, I think it's important to make a distinction between pleasure and happiness, especially since we've been discussing addiction. These two experiences are completely different in nature. The experience of pleasure is temporary, sometimes even momentary. It doesn't last and is basically over as soon as we finish engaging in the activity designed to create it. In the case of drugs, the experience of pleasure ends as soon as the drug exits the brain. As previously discussed, drugs promise happiness, but only deliver misery in the end. The temporary experience of pleasure is mistaken for happiness as the person is lied to and believes their quality of life is being enhanced by the drug. It's important to create experiences of pleasure in life, but this has to be accomplished in the right manner. In the previous discussion on substance abuse, the importance of stimulating the pleasure receptors in the brain using positive activities was highlighted. The regular creation of the experience of pleasure is important because it helps offset the negative things that happen in life, induces positive mood states, and are great outlets for anxiety build up. But again, the pleasure produced from activities, whether negative or positive, is only short lived because it's connected directly to an activity that's short lived. A good example is a really good meal. Very tasty sweet and savory foods stimulate the pleasure receptors very strongly and, because of their power, can end up becoming addictive. A favorite meal, especially if it hasn't been eaten in a while, will cause a very powerful reaction in the senses of sight, smell and taste and will cause a corresponding reaction in the reward circuitry in the brain. The resulting pleasure of that meal will be very strong, but as soon as you have eaten the last bite, the sensation of pleasure will be on its way to being over. Pleasure, even if pursued through good methods, will never produce happiness because the experience of pleasure is only temporary. This means that, if a person becomes confused and believes happiness is produced from the constant pursuit of pleasure, even good things like food, money, sex and relationships can be turned into drugs. It's very important to understand that, if we become dependent on anything outside of ourselves for our well-being, we will only experience suffering. This is the nature of addiction in any form.

The pursuit of happiness needs to be where a person puts their predominant energy and drive in life, but it needs to be defined just where happiness comes from. Happiness is only attained through the hard work it takes to succeed in goal accomplishment. What happens when we work towards achieving a goal? Obstacles and barriers appear before us, threatening to stop our efforts. In order to continue moving forward we have to block the doubts and continue to reinforce the belief in ourselves. We have to dig down further and work even harder which takes perseverance, discipline and learning new skills. All the while, our continued efforts are sustained by the belief that we can and will overcome the problem that faces us and the belief that we do have what it takes to succeed. All the positive qualities of character that are necessary for a person to be successful in life are made to grow stronger by facing the adversity posed by the obstacle. When the barrier is finally overcome, the person is stronger than before and continues to march towards the sought after goal with even greater confidence. The intrinsic quality of their character has become elevated along with their world and self-views.

As they steadily continue on the path towards their goal and continue to overcome the inevitable challenges, the person one day finds themselves at the summit. And, as they plant the flag on the top of that mountain, they will experience one of the most exhilarating experiences of pleasure that exists. However, the luster of even a long sought after goal soon starts wearing off after it's been completed. The final act of actually grasping the object of the goal in our hands isn't what makes us happy. It only produces a temporary experience of pleasure. So what creates the experience of happiness? Happiness comes from the strength and power gained on the journey towards our goals. All objects of success fade with time, but the intrinsic qualities forged from the adversity faced along the way never leave us. This is the difference between pleasure and happiness. Pleasure is the direct byproduct of the sensory experience of things that occur outside of us. Happiness is the direct byproduct of the quality of the character we build within ourselves. These are intrinsic qualities that can't be taken away from us and don't lose their luster over time if we continue to use them. In short, happiness comes from knowing we can succeed. This is the very same positive belief system that has been extolled all along. To review, that belief system is:

Good things happen in this world and they are supposed to happen to me and I have what it takes to make them happen.

When this belief system is fully integrated into the subconscious mind and the person continues to challenge themselves and succeed in goal accomplishment, they will truly know what happiness is. Happiness is a mood state that's accumulated and attained through the sustained hard work and effort required to reach a destination. The internal experience of happiness grows each time a person strengthens the above belief system and the associated intrinsic characteristics that emanate from it when faced with the adversity that comes from pursuing and attaining goals. The more powerful a person's positive belief system is, the happier they are.

The following three charts illustrate some of the main points contained in this chapter. All of the charts and graphs depicted in this work are reproductions of what I use in treatment sessions. Over time, I have found that visual reinforcement of these important concepts speeds up the learning process.

Process of Tolerance/Addiction

Brain Cell

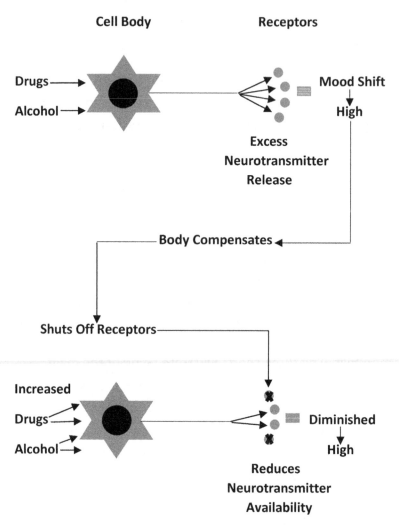

The body continues to work towards restoring system balance as the user consumes more drugs. Brain damage is occurring.

Belief System Intensification

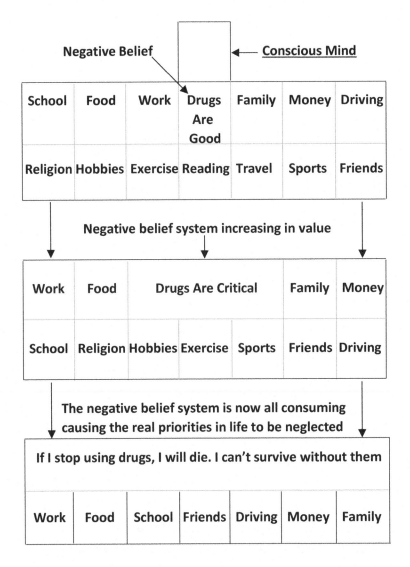

If not stopped, any negative belief system will go through these three stages of intensification.

Changing a Belief System

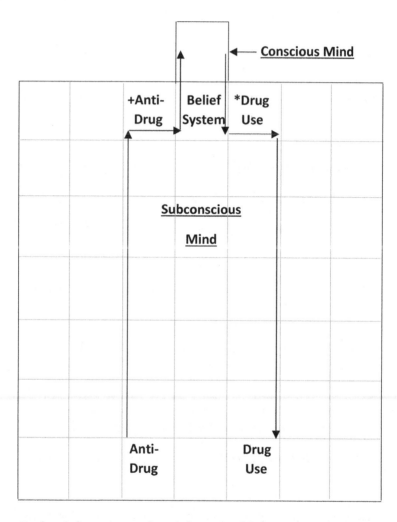

Conscious Mind

+Anti-Drug   Belief System   *Drug Use

Subconscious Mind

Anti-Drug   Drug Use

+Each reinforcement of anti-drug use thinking and action strengthens this part of the mind and pulls it progressively up to the top.

*Each rejection of drug use thinking and action weakens it and pushes it progressively down to the bottom.

Chapter 6: The Process of Change

Having read the information and concepts presented in this discussion up to this point, you will have a good idea about how to apply these principles in your own life. The basics on how to identify and correct negative mindsets are especially highlighted in the case studies reviewed so far. We will now move towards outlining the exact process in more detail. This part of the discussion will start focusing more on how you can treat yourself by laying out the process step by step. The first step is to identify the negative patterns in your life. Look for any repeated themes, actions, moods or relationships that are problematic. Ask the questions: "Where is there reoccurring failure in my life?" and, "When, where, how and with whom?" These are the first questions to ask. Most people have a very good grasp on how this occurs for them when they begin treatment. They already have a well-defined view of what their presenting problems are. This first step is the easiest. We don't have to look far or very hard to see the outward impact of the problems in our lives. Writing is a very important part of this self-analysis. You will want to get out a notepad and start writing down your thoughts when you begin to follow the guidelines presented. As noted already, the first step is problem identification. In order to focus on the steps of the process more effectively, we will once again look at a case example.

Presenting problem identification- This is a 56-year-old woman who entered treatment with her mood described as primarily anxious with some intermittent depression. She had decreased sleep and appetite, as well as disturbed short-term memory and concentration. She reported that she also had developed panic attacks while driving. The fear of driving had gotten so bad that even local driving would trigger this severe reaction. She presented with family stressors with a mother in bad health who was living in another state. She described having increasing worry about the situation her mother was in because she was legally blind and living alone. This client spoke about talking by phone with her mother six to seven times daily and that the mood of the contacts had gotten increasingly distressing. After the calls were done, she was having increasing anxiety and depression and now was dreading the daily interactions with her mother. Before her problems with driving developed, she would make the trip to visit her mother at least four times a year by herself. Due to the growing phobia attached to driving, she was unable to make the trip anymore. This client reported that she had become very physically ill before and during the last trip she made, even though she had a relative drive her the whole way there and back. She entered treatment because her mood and daily functioning had become severely impacted. This is when most people enter treatment because they are in so much emotional pain that they start thinking they can't live like this anymore. At the very beginning of treatment, she had a very good grasp on her presenting problems. She understood the current, here and now, external triggering issues and how they were affecting her mood. This client, at this early stage in treatment, thought her driving problems were completely separate from her family problems. She had no idea that they were directly connected because her problems with driving didn't surface until about six months after she returned home from the last trip in which she was able to drive by herself to see her mother. All she knew was how bad she felt and how badly she wanted to feel better. The next step in her treatment was to get her acquainted with her past and her subconscious mind.

The second step in treatment is to now look back into your history. In treatment, the therapist would direct this step, but anyone can do this on their own, using a notepad and following the guidelines. The questions here should be: "What am I afraid of?", "What thoughts and emotions are my current problems triggering in me?" and, "When, where, how and with whom have I felt this way before?" Anxiety, which is always the first mood disturbance created by any problem, is connected to fear which comes from a belief we hold to be true. At this point, we will return to our case study.

Examining the past and making connections- The problematic events with this woman's mother, worsening mood and inability to drive were causing her thought process to chronically revolve around worry. Because of the repeated adverse event exposure, she had developed the anticipatory state in her mind that bad things were going to keep happening and there was nothing she could do to stop them. This belief, and the fear radiating from it, was being strengthened daily with every phone conversation with her mother and every panic attack she had while attempting to drive her car. The fear and anxiety were growing daily. Because of this mounting expectation that, inevitably, something bad was going to happen to her or her mother, she was losing increasing control of her life. She was now focused in treatment to explore her past and remember when she had felt this way before. When, where, how and with whom? More than likely, this wasn't the first time in her life she felt this out of control.

As soon as we began exploring her childhood, we discovered when she first experienced being out of control. She identified a violent, alcoholic father who committed domestic violence in the home. She reported witnessing chronic parental fighting that would escalate to the point where her father would physically assault her mother. We had now isolated and lifted out of her subconscious mind the origin experiences that occurred early on in her life. These were the beginnings of her being caused to live in an anticipatory state that very bad things would continue to happen and there was utterly nothing she could do to stop them. Her thinking had shifted, her belief systems were formed, and her perception of reality became distorted at this early juncture in her life. Immediately, she began making the connections between then and now in her life. This was the point in treatment when she started consciously awakening to her real core problems. Her conscious mind was able to begin seeing the parallels between her past and the present condition of her life. The people, places, time and situations were different, but she was currently in the same out of control position and feeling the same way emotionally as she did back in her childhood. Remember, the subconscious mind doesn't distinguish time, place or person, it only operates on themes of learning. We didn't stop the review of her past after reviewing her childhood and capturing the origin experiences. It's very important to continue the exploration because there's the very real probability that these themes have been repeated many times since the origin experience. And, as we moved forward in her treatment, it became clear that this was the exact case in her situation.

The past exploration should continue to examine experiences from grade school through high school and continuing on up until the present. Again, to aid in your own self-analysis, you should write these down as your mind reflects back. Writing your thoughts and feelings down helps to stimulate the memory and keeps a permanent record so that you can go back and review it. As I moved forward with this client, she described having academic struggles early on in school due to problems sustaining attention. However, she did manage to stay away from drugs and alcohol. Some people, because of what they've gone through with an alcoholic parent, develop a deep commitment to never use substances in their own life. She did drop out of school early and had her first child at the age of sixteen.

This highlights a common pattern that I've seen over the years of adolescents coming from damaged, abusive homes. They tend to leave the family of origin as soon as they can. Typically, they will get involved in a relationship that acts as the vehicle to take them away from the chaos they've endured for far too long. Unfortunately, this woman didn't realize at the time that her subconscious mind had selected a frightening duplicate of her father. She thought she was running away from the abuse, but only managed to run right back into its arms. She ended up marrying him at the age of eighteen and the marriage was characterized by his alcoholism and violence towards herself and her son. After tolerating his abuse for fifteen years, she finally divorced him. She remarried a couple of years later, but her second marriage was no better than the first. This marriage was tolerated for another eleven years before she divorced him.

At this point in her exploration, she was easily able to see the repeated cycles that were occurring in her life. Her subconscious mind was reproducing her family of origin over and over again. She realized that she had tried to escape her home of origin a long time ago, but her subconscious mind had brought it along with her. However, her conscious mind was now strengthening its ability to see the parallels between her past and present situations. It was waking up to the truth that she had never stopped living in fear, even though she was long removed from the environment that had created this state in the first place. Her conscious mind was now rapidly making the connections and becoming aware of why she had continued to fall into abusive relationship and marriage cycles.

But how do all these past experiences apply to her current situation? What's the connection? At first glance, they don't appear to fit, but they do. The time, place and situation that her current problems were occurring in were different, but the position she found herself in was the same as it was in her past. We have previously discussed how the subconscious mind will look to continue to create conditions that will fulfill the goal it believes that you want. It will use whatever resources it can find to make the goal come true. This client's self-view and world-view were negatively shaped back in her childhood and then reinforced in her two subsequent marriages. And now, even at 56 years of age, she still carried around the same belief systems. Her subconscious mind had integrated them as truths over fifty years ago, before her conscious mind was fully developed. Despite several episodes of psychotherapy and multiple trials of anti-depressant medication in the past, her conscious mind had not awakened to what was causing her unending cycles of misery. At the present time in her life, her subconscious mind was using the situation with her mother to accomplish the goal of bad things continuing to occur in her life and insuring that she was powerless to do anything about it. However, now she was armed with the knowledge about the origins of the real cause of her current struggles and that they were rooted in her past. She was continuing to carry around and operate her life with wrong information that had continued to find expression in her life over and over again. She now had identified the real problem and was beginning to understand that she didn't have to continue to live this way. A firm belief formed that she could make changes to relieve and eventually remove her troubles.

This brings us to the third step of the process which comes from developing the conscious realization that the true problem isn't outside of the person, but is actually inside of the person's mind. The individual understands that the root problem is false learning and that anything learned can be unlearned. To get well, the person now realizes that they have to focus their efforts of change on their own mind in order to change the outcome of their outside world. Finally, the mystery of the continuing cycles of misery has been solved because an identifiable cause has been discovered. Once you identify and understand the cause, the conscious mind can start the process of extinguishing the false learning and convincing the subconscious mind to integrate the correct learning. The conscious mind can now go about the business of teaching the subconscious mind the real truth:

I do have the ability to positively change the quality of my life.

Reinforced now is the concept that there was never anything wrong with her. Rather, she was made to feel bad about herself by other people and situations that weren't her fault. The process of depersonalizing the experiences occurs within the mind which starts separating the past from the present. The conscious mind now begins teaching the subconscious mind to let go of the wrong information from the past and to accept the right information that now needs to be applied in life to achieve good outcomes. The concept becomes very clear because it has been traced back in the person's life and they can plainly see it operating over and over again. The conscious mind, which is the only part of the mind that operates with logic, can see it very clearly. It can see the pattern that wrong information leads to bad outcomes and understands that operating with the right information will lead to good outcomes. This is a basic truth that anyone understands if they use the logic of their conscious mind. Correction within the mind can only take place when the person's conscious mind awakens and sees that this has been the problem all along. We will now return to our case study and examine the next step in the treatment process.

The conscious mind fully awakens- This client had entered treatment thinking that her driving problems weren't connected to her fears associated with her mother. She didn't understand why she had, all of a sudden, developed a phobia directly related to driving a car. She had never had a problem with driving in her life and had never been in an accident that could've rationally explained such a fear. A big part of her conscious awakening, and ultimately fixing her current presenting problems, was discovering how her inability to drive was a direct result of the distress over her mother. As previously outlined, she spoke with her mother multiple times daily. Her mother was elderly, legally blind, and living on her own. She had tried to get her mother to leave her home and come live with her, or possibly move into an assisted living facility, but her mother refused to move. Over the past couple of years, the nature of the phone calls with her mother had gotten increasingly dark and negative. She would leave each phone contact increasingly upset. At the time she entered treatment, she now dreaded each day and the impending phone calls from her mother. As the days wore on, her anxiety grew because the situation fit right into her core negative belief systems. Her subconscious mind built on this situation, causing her mind to create ever worsening scenarios of the fates that could befall her mother.

It has previously been pointed out, in the discussion on substance abuse, how the subconscious mind will continue to increasingly catastrophize a negative belief until it becomes merged with the survival mechanism within the human system. If not stopped by the conscious mind, this anticipation of bad outcome will eventually become equated with death. This happens with all false belief systems and this exact process had been steadily evolving in her mind. What was occurring on a subconscious level was that, if it feels this bad just talking to her on the phone, how terrible will it be if I actually go there and see her? Surely something awful and horrible will happen. As referred to earlier, she had been able to make the sixteen hour round trip drive by herself, without problem, up until two years ago. Over the past year and a half, she had been experiencing increasing fear while driving and now was at the point where even driving locally was causing her great difficulty. Panic attacks had developed while driving and she was only able to go visit her mother with someone else driving. However, the fears didn't subside and she soon developed panic reactions, even though she was just a passenger in the car. On her last trip out to see her mother, she had become physically ill the week before the trip and during the drive which almost caused her to abort the journey and go back home. Can you see the progression that is occurring here? It was very important for her to see what was happening to her and to what lengths her subconscious mind would go to stop her from seeing her mother. Her subconscious mind was operating with the full belief that, if she went out to see her mother, something horrible was going to happen. It had initially attached this intense fear to driving a car to the extent that she could no longer make the drive herself. But what was her response to the problem? She got someone else to do the drive for her. And then what happened next? She had gotten very physically ill just before and during the trip. So sick, that she almost had to turn back and go home. Would her subconscious mind go that far in order to prevent her from going somewhere that it felt she would be in imminent danger? The answer is that it will, and it did, in her situation. If the conscious mind is used to examine the progression of what was happening to her, what is the logical conclusion about what would occur next if she continued to find a way to get to her mother's? She logically projected the process forward and made the correct conclusion that she would become so physically ill that she wouldn't even be able to leave her home in order to get in the car.

The conscious mind needs to make these types of connections so that it can identify what the real problems are. Without coming to this awareness herself, she wouldn't have been able to make the proper connections and figure out the real problem she was facing. She had to know what to fix in order to fix it. Her subconscious mind was operating on a false belief that was distorting her perception, mood and actions. The end result being that she was getting exactly what she expected, anticipated and feared in the first place. Something bad was indeed continuing to happen to her, but it was her own mind that was creating it.

The conscious mind takes control- At this point in her treatment she was fully awake and aware. Her conscious mind was now in position to take control of the real problem and make the necessary changes. It had only taken a few sessions for this client to get her mind into this position and now she was ready to do something about her problems, supported by the growing belief that she could. Anyone on their own, following these same guidelines, can achieve the same results in the same amount of time.

All of the presenting problems she faced were directly caused by the extreme threat level created by the daily contacts with her mother. These contacts had caused her subconscious mind to use them as a way to express outwardly the continual state of anticipation she carried inside of her that bad things would continue to appear in her life. To review, when this is the belief system a person carries within them, the subconscious mind is always looking for the best way to manifest this goal. Her subconscious mind, over a two-year period, had turned the contacts with her mother into a huge threat that had definitely moved towards being perceived as life threatening. She now began the process of correction by attacking the root of the problem and had to change the perception of contact with her mother, both on the phone and in person. Her conscious mind had to start removing the threat of these contacts and teach the subconscious mind to look at them in a good way. By getting the subconscious mind to accept that contact with her mother was a good thing, and nothing to be feared, it would mobilize every effort to support her getting out to visit her mother. It would release its attachment of fear to driving so that she could once again make the trip herself. In order to successfully accomplish this change, she had to convince her subconscious mind to let go of her inherited origin belief system that the world is a bad place where bad things happen and there's nothing that can be done to stop them. She had to get her subconscious mind to stop operating with the wrong information and had to get it to start operating with the right belief system. The next step in the process of treatment is activating change where the person starts taking control and taking action.

Activation- Here is the plan of empowerment that this client followed.

1. She contacted social services in the state where her mother lived and made arrangements to get her mother engaged in a supportive program for senior citizens.

2. She contacted her mother's Medicare insurance and her primary care doctor to get a visiting nurses program coming out to the home. These two steps eased her mind because she knew that people were involved with her mother, could assess her condition and help her if needed.

3. She kept in contact with her mother's primary care doctor and made sure what her mother's medical care plan was and that it was being followed through.

4. She continued to encourage her mother to open up to the idea of coming to live with her, but developed a back-up plan in case her mother's condition deteriorated more and she needed to be placed in some level of assisted care. If needed, she would get power of attorney, or guardianship, through the probate court to make medical decisions for her mother.

5. She limited the number and duration of contacts with her mother per day, systematically decreasing them to eventually one per day. Reducing the trigger events was an integral part of reducing their threat level and increasing her ability to turn them into good events.

6. She closely watched her thoughts and mood while talking to her mother. Whenever she caught either going negative, she immediately countered with internal, positive self-talk to block her subconscious mind from catastrophizing the experience. Anytime we are talking to ourselves, it's our conscious mind communicating with the subconscious mind. Ultimately, the way the conscious mind convinces the subconscious mind of the real truth is by opening up and sustaining this dialogue between the two. As soon as she recognized the negative mind, she used the mental image of a stop sign to stop the negative mental process and then redirected her mind to silently repeat soothing, calming phrases that she had developed. She kept a picture by her, while on the phone, of a soothing landscape as a constant reminder when she looked at it to stay calm. She also watched her breathing closely, knowing that increased breathing rate is associated with increased fear. She worked on controlling and regulating her breathing while on the phone. The design of the specific mechanisms or tools used by each person is up to their own personal preference of what clicks for them. Everyone comes up with their own unique phrases, images or objects and the manner in which they are applied. The only constant should be that they

communicate a soothing message to the whole mental system, that everything is okay and that they're safe. This is important because the subconscious mind is the one reacting strongly and telling the person that they need to be very, very afraid. The subconscious mind is the child who is upset and afraid. The conscious mind is the parent who intervenes and makes the child believe that everything will be alright and that there's nothing to be afraid of. This is how the conscious mind steps in and takes control of the process, blocks the negative mind and inserts and reinforces the positive mind. The conscious mind is correcting the perception of the event, getting the subconscious mind to see it for what it really is, thereby eliminating the threat level. And, because the mood mirrors what the mind believes to be true, the high level of anxiety created by the perceived fear will be eliminated.

7. She worked on building, in her mind, a state of anticipating the phone calls with good expectations. She had to create and strengthen the reasons why it was good for her to talk with her mother by phone and also to go out to visit her. The truth is, we can talk ourselves into anything, either good or bad. She had to now talk herself into looking forward to her contacts with her mother, instead of dreading them. Again, to review an important concept, the key to getting the subconscious mind to believe anything is through the process of repetition. Any concept or experience, repeated enough, will be accepted and integrated into the subconscious mind as a truth. The subconscious mind is built to be a follower because it

doesn't look at information in terms of true or false. The conscious mind, on the other hand, is built to be a leader because it has the capability to analyze information and accept or reject it based on validity. The subconscious mind will follow the conscious mind's correction and direction, if demanded enough times. It has to be told what is right and what is wrong. The conscious mind has to take control of this process otherwise the person is at risk of the subconscious mind getting ahold of the wrong information, making decisions based on it, and causing a whole lot of trouble.

8. As part of reinforcing her new view of the contacts with her mother, she wrote down a list of all the reasons why it was good for her and her mother to have contact. She kept that list out in the open where she could see it and read it multiple times per day. She wrote down a positive statement, in her own style, about how she would enjoy her time with her mother and repeated this multiple times daily. In addition, she came up with and wrote down the new positive world and self-views she wanted to operate with in her life. She taped copies of this around her home so that she couldn't avoid running into them throughout the day. She stopped every time she saw one and repeated it with great conviction to herself. I've had clients actually tape this message to the top of their bedroom ceiling so that this was the first thing they saw every day. I've also had clients set an alarm in their cell phones with this statement as the message so that they could have an additional method to create the type of repetition that is

required to retrain the subconscious mind. Other methods that I advise clients to add are viewing inspirational videos and movies, reading books with the same theme and listening to music that evokes the same emotion.

You should be getting the idea now. You need to **flood** the subconscious mind with the new theme, the new learning, the new belief system, in any and all the methods you can find and develop. The more you flood it, the faster it will receive and integrate the new learning. You should begin and end your day with exposure to it and prompt your mind to return to it as many times as possible in between.

9. During the day, whenever she caught her thoughts or mood going negative, she made the effort to stop it and redirect her mind back to the positive correction. She began actively making her mind look at the positives of people and situations and not allowing her subconscious mind to look for problems or trouble. She kept a running list of all the good that was going on in her life, even down to basics such as having a place to live, food to eat, clothes to wear, etc. She read this list every day and added to it whenever she thought of a new item. The function of this was to overwhelm the subconscious mind with irrefutable evidence of how many good things were happening in her life. This goes directly to supporting the new, positive belief system she wanted integrated into her subconscious mind. Another way of reinforcing this theme is to review each day at the end and highlight all the good things that

happened. The beginning of each day should be started repeating something like this:

Today is going to be a great day and no matter what comes my way, I will maintain a positive attitude.

Conversely, one should strive to end each day before going to sleep with the same thought, but changing one word:

Tomorrow is going to be a great day and no matter what comes my way, I will maintain a positive attitude.

10. Consciously, she now understood where her fear of driving had come from and how irrational it was. With her conscious mind now taking control, she proceeded to reinstitute the belief that driving is good and safe. Just a little over two years ago, she had fully understood in her mind that driving enhanced the quality of her life by giving her independence. She realized that, if she continued to allow her subconscious mind to carry a belief that driving was going to deliver her into harm's way, she would never drive again and would lose a great deal of freedom in her life. Therefore, the actual truth was that the quality of her life would go down, not up. She now understood that her subconscious mind was operating under the opposite belief and had to be stopped. Knowing the core problem, her conscious mind was able to use its grasp of logic to quickly teach the subconscious mind the truth and remove her fear of driving. I have seen, many times in treatment, where this realization alone is enough to cause the subconscious mind to almost immediately let go of false

belief systems and the fear that had been associated with them. I have witnessed some clients accomplish this in only one session. In this woman's case, as soon as she realized what was causing her difficulties driving, she made the internal correction and was driving without panic attacks. By following this plan, she was able to successfully achieve the outcome she had sought when she first entered treatment. Her total time in treatment was two months. This is very rapid progress, but her case demonstrates how quickly a person can overcome paralyzing fear by activating the conscious mind.

It's very important for people who enter treatment to know that they may have carried around their negative belief systems for years, but it doesn't take years to correct them. The subconscious mind is very powerful, but highly suggestible and it will follow the demands of the conscious mind. I tell clients, especially after they have done the historical work to trace the origins of their current problems, that it may have taken years for the problem to develop, but it can take only weeks to correct it, depending on how hard they work. Many clients get discouraged after the discovery phase and will actually say: "I'm forty years old now, will it take another forty for me to get better?" I tell them, at this point, that I have seen people accomplish the task of retraining and restructuring the subconscious mind in the matter of weeks. Certainly, within a year, one can become a completely different person in terms of mind, mood and action. It's very important to hear this because I have found that most people who enter treatment have serious doubts about whether they'll ever be happy in their lives. After reviewing the above case study, you can see that there is hard work involved, but this is what it takes to retrain the mind and get it back to functioning the way it should with the conscious mind in control, doing its job, and the subconscious mind following its lead. Continued, repetitive practice of the mental process outlined will yield results. It's inevitable because of how the mind is structured. The subconscious mind has to accept and integrate the positive constructs if demanded enough times by the conscious mind. The absolute truth is that:

We are what we repeatedly think. The quality of our outer life is the direct result of the quality of our inner life, which is our mind.

At this time, the process or method of treatment will be broken down into its simplest terms. It is as follows:

1. Identify the negative or false beliefs that need to be changed. Explore history to identify the origin experiences. There have only been a rare handful of cases in my career where the client wasn't able to isolate their origin experiences. These were all cases where childhood sexual abuse was highly suspected, but the memories were so walled off that the client couldn't retrieve them, or it wasn't in their best interests to try and recover them. However, this discovery wasn't necessary for them to move forward in treatment.

2. Raise conscious awareness on the negative mind. Practice mindfulness and constantly watch the thought process throughout the day.

3. At the earliest recognition of negative thinking, step in with the conscious mind and stop it. Develop a mental image like a stop sign, or phrase, and use it to break the negative thought process. This is the first part that people get good at.

4. Redirect the mind to the positive thinking that you want in its place. Repeat the positive thoughts in the mind and explanations of why the one is false and the other is true. This is the opening of the dialogue between the conscious mind and subconscious mind. This is where the teaching and retraining takes place.

5. Repeatedly expose the subconscious mind to the positive belief system. The world is good, people are good, good things are supposed to happen to me and I can make them happen. Use your own unique style to make this statement your own.

6. Set goals, develop action steps to accomplish them and then work towards achieving them. Make sure the goals are attainable and tailored to your own specific problem areas. It doesn't matter how big the goals are, all that matters is that you set them and then follow through with the steps to accomplish them. This part of the process is critical because it provides objective evidence to the subconscious mind that the positive belief system you've

been pouring into it is true. It responds something like this when a goal is completed: "What you've been telling me must be true because it just happened." This outward confirmation works very powerfully to counteract the negative belief system that the subconscious mind has been holding onto and believes to be true. Whenever a goal is achieved, it reinforces the belief that good things do happen and you have the ability to make them happen. The idea is to create, "I did it.", moments to back up what you've been repeating over and over again to your subconscious mind.

This part of the process can be better illustrated by going over another case example. This case is different because this man had a positive belief system that was altered in an instant by a tragic accident. The origin experience that turned his belief systems negative occurred much later in his life. This client entered treatment about a month after being involved in a terrible car accident. He was working one snowy February day at his job as a garbage truck driver. The road conditions were bad and he was struck head on by a car that lost control. The driver of the car was severely injured and the client was trapped in his truck due to the damage. Because the other driver's injuries were life threatening, the first responders worked on this driver first. The client had to sit with his own injuries and watch them try to save this other man. Because of how a garbage truck's front end and driver's compartment is structured, it was like the other car's windshield was literally a few feet away. He could see everything right up to the moment when they pronounced him dead. This client ended up with significant injuries to his hands, legs, back and neck. However, another serious injury had occurred which wasn't visible at the scene of the accident. It manifested about a week later after he was released from the hospital and was driven home by his wife. On the way home, he experienced a terrifying emotional reaction so severe that his wife had to pull off to the side of the road. He had obviously been traumatized by the accident and was suffering from PTSD. During the first session, he reported that he couldn't drive a car anymore and that the trauma reactions were so bad as a passenger that he could barely be driven by his wife to medical appointments because he would physically jerk and jump throughout the whole ride. It was such a distraction to his wife that he was afraid it would cause her to get in an accident. His hands were pretty badly injured in the accident and were still healing when he first entered treatment. There was no way he could drive at that time because of his hands, but he knew they would heal and wanted to start treatment to try and get control of his anxiety connected to driving.

In the blink of an eye, this man's whole world changed. He liked his life up until the time of the accident. He had a good job, good marriage and a nice house. He was content with his life, but that all turned upside down after the accident. There were many material and physical losses. He was unable to work and his income was down because of this. He had never worried much about money, but now he had financial issues. He had lost a great deal of independence because of the physical injuries and had to rely on family to take care of him in a lot of ways while his body healed. However, his greatest sense of worry was connected to what had happened to his mind. Would he ever drive again? Would he ever be able to return to his job? What would they do financially if he couldn't work again? Would he lose his house? Would he be able to provide for his family? All because of this one instant in time and the subsequent losses, his mind had been turned completely negative. In addition, he talked about not being able to get the events of the accident out of his mind, both the split second of the impact and crash and then seeing the dead driver in the car right in front of him. He had repeated nightmares about this and now was afraid to go to sleep at night. Whenever he got into a car to go to an appointment, he felt as if he was going to come out of his skin for fear of going through another accident.

His mind was now in a constant anticipatory state of terrible things continuing to happen and there was nothing he could do to stop them. As a result, his mood was filled with constant anxiety that would escalate quickly to severe panic attacks while in a car because he was afraid for his life. In fact, the panic attacks had been growing and were now triggered by his car racing video games and movies or television shows with car action scenes in them. Depression had also been developing as he had been increasingly wondering if he would ever recover and live the life he had prior to the accident. His world-view and self-view, which had been positive right before the accident, were now both negative. The world was now a bad place where terrible things happen, people die, and there's nothing that can be done to prevent it from happening. This was the exact accident experience and now it was his integrated belief system which would become his life goal if he didn't stop it. This case shows how one adverse experience, if powerful enough, can instantaneously change a person's belief systems. The greatest fear, obviously, was connected to driving which was the biggest obstacle in regaining the belief that, despite the accident, he could live a good, successful and happy life again. He needed to regain his ability to drive without fear. So, taking the first step in the process listed above, we have:

Identify the negative or false belief system that needs to be changed in detail. **If I drive again, either myself or someone else will die.**

Not much work needs to be done in past exploration and analysis. This client fully knows the origin experience and knows what it did to his thinking. He knows why he is deathly afraid to be in a car. One of the other differences in this case is that to have a great fear of being in a vehicle after such a terrible and tragic accident is fully understandable. The learning from this experience doesn't defy logic.

The second step of the process is fulfilled. His conscious mind is fully awake and has identified the negative belief system that is causing his inability to drive. He is all too aware of its presence and interference in his life.

The rest of the steps involve the actual activation of the treatment plan that was developed to help him. Once his body healed sufficiently, a systematic plan was implemented which involved the client exposing himself to driving one little step at a time. Small goals were set and then the steps were outlined that he would use to accomplish the goal. As he mastered his anxiety at each step, he would then create the next goal which was a little more challenging than the one before it. This process is called desensitization. He started just sitting in the car behind the wheel and worked on controlling the trauma reaction. When he could sit behind the wheel without a panic attack and self-rate the anxiety at no more than a five on a scale of zero to ten with ten the worst, he then moved on to starting the car up and backing it down the driveway and then pulling it back to the top. When the anxiety was controlled here, he moved onto having his wife take him to an empty parking lot where he drove around the parking lot. He wasn't ready to go out into the subdivision street yet because he would have to face an oncoming car in the other lane which was his biggest fear. Next, he had his wife drive a car slowly by his car in the empty parking lot until he had learned how to control his anxiety in the most threatening situation for him.

The next step was a huge step in his progress towards overcoming his fears. This one was backing the car into the subdivision street and then driving around the subdivision.

At the end of his treatment, he pointed to this step as the most crucial to overcome. He felt that, once he had been able to tolerate another car passing by him in the opposite lane, he knew he'd be able to drive again. He successfully conquered this step and then successively desensitized his fear of driving even further by going on main roads that had progressively faster speed limits. Within three months of the day he entered treatment, he drove to his session by himself. This had been his long range goal when he had started the desensitization program.

In order to accomplish this goal, he had to convince his subconscious mind to re-integrate what he believed to be true about driving before the accident. Prior to the accident, he never gave a second thought to either driving his personal car or his work truck because he had no reason to. At that time, driving was seen as safe and as automatic as breathing every day. By breaking his long-term goal down into small steps that he determined were attainable, he was able to systematically get his subconscious mind to let go of the belief that, if he drove his car again, he or someone else would die. He was able to show his subconscious mind the truth that, just because the accident occurred, it didn't mean that it would happen again. Repeating over and over again throughout the day that driving is safe was not enough to achieve his goal. He had to back up what he was teaching his subconscious mind with action. This is what is so important about setting goals and coming up with an action plan to work towards them. As he completed each step in his action plan, his confidence in his abilities grew, as did the positive belief about driving. This reduced the fear enough to proceed to the next step in the plan. The confidence that grows is: "If I could do that, then I can do this." Each successful step strengthens the overall belief system that good things do happen to me and I know I can make them happen again.

This man became increasing empowered in this belief with each step that was completed on his way towards his goal. In this manner, he was able to take control of his life and not allow the fear generated from a past event to dictate how he thought, felt and acted. It's important to add here that he was able to accomplish this type of progress in treatment without the aid of any psychiatric medication. He wasn't able to use medication because, in order to return to his job as a garbage truck driver, he couldn't be on any type of psychiatric medication. This makes what he was able to accomplish, in such a short period of time, even more impressive.

This client used all the same techniques outlined in the previous case example, but tailored to his own unique presenting problems. He flooded his subconscious mind with the positive belief about driving, and, whenever he caught his subconscious mind using the traumatized version or perseverating on memories of the accident, he intervened with his conscious mind to stop it and get it back on the positive track. Because this negative looping can be so powerful and hard to stop, it becomes very hard at times to just stop it mentally and get it to switch over to a positive loop. The subconscious mind will strongly resist your efforts to let it go. Just like a dog with a bone, the more you wrestle with it to let it go, the harder it bites down to keep it. This is when distraction techniques can be very helpful. The idea behind this technique is busying yourself with some other activity to change the channel in your mind. Most people have the most trouble with the mind becoming engrossed with negative thoughts when they're idle. The best thing to do is to get up and move physically and choose something else to do. It should involve mental and physical activity for best results. For example, reading a book is usually not active enough to distract the mind away from its negative obsessions.

Because this client was unable to work, he had big blocks of idle time during which his mind would go completely negative. This was a huge barrier in the beginning and he had to find a way to stop his mind from feeding the fear. To help himself, he developed a set of distraction techniques. Whenever he found his mind in this negative idle state, he would go for a walk, or exercise. When his hands recovered, he would attend to unfinished home maintenance tasks around the house and did the same outside the house. He made a list of tasks and activities he could do and made a daily schedule to follow. It was a challenge because he was off of work, but he managed to keep as busy as possible. This effectively reduced the amount of idle time he had during the day which reduced the amount of negative perseveration. The more time a person spends in productive activities, the more time their mind spends in positive states and then the better their mood is. Healthy activities of distraction help greatly towards the ultimate goal of restructuring the subconscious mind to become increasingly positive. Again, these were positive action steps that worked towards reinforcing the theme of empowerment within him. Yes, there is something I can do about my problems. Yes, I can take action and make positive changes in my life. You want to strengthen I can, I can, I can in thought, word and deed continually.

Along with the above tools, he used a relaxation technique combined with positive affirmations and positive visualization. He used this mental exercise two to three times daily and specifically used it to relax his anxiety level just before he went out on his driving steps. The exact exercise is outlined in a later chapter. For our purposes here, I want to focus on how he used visualization to assist him in achieving his goals. The relaxation exercise is designed to induce a calm mental, emotional and physical state. When this state is accomplished, you aren't centered in the conscious mind anymore because the senses are almost turned off. When we sleep, our conscious mind is turned off because the senses are turned off. At night, when we are sleeping, we are right in the midst of our subconscious mind which never sleeps. In a very deeply calmed and relaxed state, the conscious mind is hovering right above the sleep state. In fact, it's teetering right on that line. Most people find that if they lie down and do this exercise, especially when they're already tired, they will cross that line and fall asleep. Therefore, when a person purposely induces this deeply relaxed state, the conscious mind is turned off and they are in the midst of their subconscious mind. Any positive statement, affirmation or visualization created at this time is powerfully received and registered by the subconscious mind. In session, I walked this client through the relaxation process and then walked him through how to use the visualization process to mentally envision himself going through the driving steps. For visualization to have its strongest effect on the subconscious mind, you must create the mental images with as much detail as possible. Vividly imagine the sights, sounds and colors, just as if you were watching this on a computer monitor or television screen. Why is visualization so effective if done correctly? To answer this question, we need to review the characteristics of the subconscious mind. This part of the mind doesn't distinguish time, place or person, but the crucial one here is time. When you repeatedly visualize yourself completing an action successfully, using ever greater detail to imagine it with, you are tricking the subconscious mind into believing it has already happened. I will repeat this concept again:

The subconscious mind actually believes the action or activity has already taken place.

Therefore, when you go to do the actual activity for real, your chances of succeeding increase dramatically. Your subconscious mind believes that you've already done this many times because it has seen it. As this client entered each phase of the current action step he was working on, his mind was familiar with it and knew what to do. His confidence was up because the fear of the unknown was reduced. His subconscious mind believed he had already been there before, so there was nothing to worry about. It was safe because it always ended well. There was no reason to believe it would end badly. His subconscious mind had seen the end of this particular scene many times before. It's very important to feel the mood of the activity while you're envisioning it in your mind. As you're going through the motion picture in your mind, you want to be full of confidence, strength, happiness, joy, calmness, courage, etc. You not only want to envision the successful completion of the activity, but also envision how you want to feel during it.

The above case example highlights the cognitive interventions, exercises and goal setting this client used to reverse the effects that a severe traumatic event had on his life. He was able to successfully convince his subconscious mind to let go of the false learning that occurred as a result of his accident and accept as truth, once again, that driving was safe and good. In the beginning of his treatment, he was barely able to be driven as a passenger in a vehicle. At the end of his treatment, he was in full control of his mental and emotional state and was driving himself everywhere.

Chapter 7: Developing a Treatment Plan

In this chapter, guidelines for how to construct your own personal history review and treatment plan will be explained.

The Questions

This is an outline of questions to direct the conscious mind to start exploring history and to identify events that were significant in shaping the belief systems, especially in childhood before it was mature enough to be aware of this psychological and emotional process. The term childhood is used to cover the years from birth to the end of high school. By doing this, your conscious mind is digging into the subconscious mind to see what is in there that is still negatively influencing your life. Write down the memories that come up in as much detail as you can. When, where, with whom, and what was happening around you? What were your feelings and reactions? As the memories come up, just let them flow and write down whatever appears. Don't steer, direct, or guide them. Take note of any strong emotional reactions if they occur. Mark these and what memories they are connected to. This always means that it is something very powerful and still affecting you to this day.

1. What was your household environment like during your childhood?

2. How would you describe your mother, what was she like back then?

3. How would you describe your father, what was he like back then?

4. How would you describe your relationship with your mother?

5. How would you describe your relationship with your father?

6. What was your parents' relationship like, what do you remember seeing?

7. What do you think were the significant events that occurred in your family during your childhood?

8. What do you think were the significant events that happened to you during your childhood?

9. When you were upset, what would you do?

10. What were your academic and social experiences like during elementary school?

11. What were your academic and social experiences like during middle school?

12. What were your academic and social experiences like during high school?

The next set of questions should focus on experiences that occur in adulthood. Romantic relationships include marriages.

13. Who have your romantic relationships been with and how have they gone?

14. How would you describe their personalities?

15. How would you describe your relationships with your children?

16. Who are your friends, how would you describe them, and what is your social life like?

17. How have jobs gone for you with regards to performance and relationships?

18. How have you done in educational efforts after high school?

19. When anxious, agitated, or depressed, what do you do to feel better?

20. What do you think are the significant events that have occurred in your adulthood?

As you are remembering, exploring, and writing down your answers to these questions, you want to look for patterns. Especially patterns from the first set of questions that connect to the second set. Do you see any parallels? If negative belief systems formed in childhood, you will see the same negative cycles that occurred in childhood continuing to play out in adulthood, just in different settings, situations, and with different people. The subconscious mind will use the false learning that occurred to continue to recreate the past and put you in the same position of harm and powerlessness.

Treatment Plan Outline

Using an actual case, we will go through and generate an outline of how to proceed with your own self-analysis and develop your own treatment plan. The first information we want to focus on is: What is this client's conscious knowledge of her presenting issues? What does she see, think, and feel about what is occurring in her life? This is followed by: What are her resulting actions? And, lastly: What is the final outcome of her choices? We want to capture what her conscious experience is of the problems she is bringing into treatment.

What is the conscious awareness of what is happening?

1. Presenting issues- This is a 22-year-old single female who is living with a male significant other. She reports relationship problems with frequent verbal fighting. She reports her mood as angry, irritable, and anxious. She denies depression, but reports her mood will shift suddenly to intense anger with resultant loss of verbal control. She is questioning whether the relationship is worth staying in.

2. Triggers of mood shift- When her significant other works with females, or they are in a setting where other females

are present, like the gym, she perceives that he is giving them attention. In addition, she becomes anxious and angry if he is out without her, at work or otherwise, and doesn't check in with her regularly to let her know where he is at.

3. Thought process- She is threatened and fears he will leave her for someone better. She believes that he is lying and cheating on her.

4. Resulting actions- She calls to check on him more than she should. She doesn't trust him and needs reports on where he is at and who he is with. She looks for inconsistencies in his reports. She believes he is lying and looks to catch him in lies. Anxiety and anger build which causes her to confront him when he comes home and a verbal fight always ensues. If they are at a place like the gym, she focuses on her significant other and the other women in the gym, looking for a problem. Her mood shifts again and she wants to leave because she doesn't feel like working out anymore. The anger will cause her to withdraw and distance from him. He then pursues her, trying to find out what happened or what he did wrong, which inevitably leads to another verbal altercation.

5. Outcome- Increasing conflict and bad experiences between them. Distrust and an increasingly negative view of him. Increasing belief that she needs to leave the relationship. Increasingly disturbed mood. The relationship is in the process of being destroyed.

Now that we have established what's happening up on the surface of her conscious experience, we need to focus on what's happening underneath in the subconscious level of her mind. It's important to shift in this direction to discover what's really guiding her thoughts, perceptions, feelings, and actions regarding the problems in her relationship. This part of the process helps guide the conscious mind to start looking inside the mind for the true source of the outward problems. The awakening begins.

What is happening in the subconscious level of the mind?

1. <u>What are the origin experiences</u>? Examination revealed there was no current evidence to shape the severe distrust she held towards her significant other. He had done nothing to cause her to hold this view of him. Review of her history quickly revealed the origins. Severe parental discord led to the divorce of her parents when she was six years old. Several years later she found out that her father had an affair while they were married. She was sexually abused by one of her mother's subsequent boyfriends and a couple family members on the father's side of the family from the ages of six to thirteen. She reported that she told her mother more than once about the abuse, but her mother did nothing about it. Her father had multiple relationships and eventually remarried. She reported that her father gave these other women much more attention than he gave her. The step-mother mentally abused her, tearing her down repeatedly.

2. <u>What are the parallels between the origin and present experiences</u>? Her beliefs and fears forged from her early abuse are attaching to the current experience, causing her to relive it. She is turning her significant other into her father and the men who sexually abused her. Females around her are being turned into her step-mother and the other women that she lost out to in competition for her father.

3. <u>What are the operating belief systems</u>? Men will ultimately hurt you, lie to you, betray you, and leave you for someone else. Women will take what belongs to you. In addition, her self-view is that she isn't good enough and doesn't measure up to other women. Something bad always comes around to ruin the good things that she has. Talking about problems doesn't work and will only cause more problems. Nothing will change.

4. <u>What needs to change</u>? Change the learned negative view of men, women, and herself to the positive view. Correct her perception of current events when faced with the identified triggers. Understand that it's a reaction from past events and the great fear that she will be hurt and rejected again. Realize that the old way of thinking and reacting doesn't apply now and is ruining her relationship. If she continues with her current actions, she will guarantee that she loses her significant other by driving him away. In the end, she will cause the very outcome she fears the most to happen. The conscious part of her mind

has to stop the subconscious part from using the past to distort her current experience.

At this point, her conscious mind is now fully aware of what the true source of her current problems is. A plan of action can now be formulated to target the root cause of her turbulent relationship and achieve her desired goals in treatment. The activation begins.

The plan of correction.

1. Write down the positive belief systems and start flooding them into the subconscious mind. Men are good, women are good, people are good, and I am good and worthy. Talking about problems is productive. I have the ability to make positive changes in my life. Repeat often.

2. Write down a specific statement affirming the good person that her significant other is. List all of his good qualities. Reinforce the evidence and facts that prove he has done nothing to justify her negative view of him. Repeat often.

3. Write down all her good qualities affirming how strong and good she is. Use this to confirm that she doesn't need anyone else to validate her. She doesn't have to prove her worth to anyone. She knows that she is talented, intelligent, and beautiful. She understands that she can't keep looking to get the validation she didn't get from her father out of her significant other. Repeat often.

4. Because her significant other is good and to be trusted, stop requiring that he check in when he is away from her. If she is at home alone while he is away, don't sit around with nothing to do. Get out of the house, go visit friends, go to the gym, etc. Keep her mind distracted and on a positive activity, preventing it from perseverating on the negative theme of distrust and that something bad is about to happen. Don't allow the fears from the past to make her anxious and angry and jump to conclusions that he will cheat on her. He is not her father and just because her father betrayed her, it doesn't mean he will. They are different people and it's a different time. She must separate the past from influencing her in the present.

5. When with him in public and around other women, use positive self-talk and distraction to redirect her thought process from attaching to the situation and making her believe it's a threatening one. Stop fearing that he will run off and have an affair with any women in her sight she has determined to be dangerous. Again, this isn't her family of origin all over again. It's a different time, place, situation, and completely different people are involved. It's not the same. When in the gym and this occurs, redirect the focus to herself and why she is there. Focus on having a great workout. Don't allow the past to ruin having a good experience in the present. Repeatedly reinforce her value as a person. Repeatedly work on removing the perceived threat from the environment.

6. When triggered and angry with her significant other, work on stopping any verbal interaction turning into a fight. Develop a plan to identify cues in herself when it's time to walk away from it and focus on calming and correcting her perception. Strip away the past influence and see if there is any legitimate evidence in the present that would justify her being angry with him. If there is, return at a later time when calm and revisit the discussion and keep it a controlled conversation. If she becomes aware of the cues that she is getting too angry again, walk away and repeat the process.

7. Involve her significant other in treatment sessions so they can focus on building their ability to communicate with each other. Work together on defining what effective communication is and identify what happens when theirs breaks down. Set aside a time once a week to sit down with her significant other and practice strengthening their communication skills. Set an agenda just like a business meeting and focus on the chosen topics. It doesn't matter what is talked about, but the priority is to focus on the process of communication. Repeat and reinforce often that talking about issues and problems is good and will help her. Repeatedly reinforce that they, as a couple, can communicate effectively and work together to accomplish goals or resolve any problems they have.

8. Practice calming the mind and mood actively with guided relaxation and meditation daily. Exercise daily. Plan and create opportunities weekly for good experiences with

her significant other to remind herself why she wants him in her life and how good they can be together.

9. Develop, pursue, and accomplish targeted goals around her career, continuing education, and physical fitness to consistently reinforce the desired positive belief system. The world is a good place, where good things happen, and they happen to her because she has the ability to make them happen.

Having the courage to enter treatment, this young woman gave herself the opportunity to walk through this process, even though it was very painful at times. During the session when we were analyzing her failed relationship with her father, she instantly saw the connection on how she was recreating it in her current relationship. Her immediate response was, "That's _____ up." It doesn't take much imagination to figure out what middle word she actually used in that short sentence. However, her response was perfect for capturing the impact on her mind when she figured out what was really going on. This was the moment of her conscious awakening, and, from there, she was able to construct a plan to save herself and her relationship. She knew exactly what she needed to do and, by following the plan, she activated her conscious mind to direct the necessary changes in her subconscious mind.

Creating Your Own Plan

What follows is a step by step guide to help you identify the real core problems that lie in your subconscious mind.

This process will lead to the restoration of the correct relationship between your conscious and subconscious minds. It will establish your conscious mind back in control of your thought process, mood, and actions. The subconscious mind will now be directed to let go of all the old, false learning from the past and replace it with the correct, positive belief systems. This process will help you develop your own treatment plan so that your conscious and subconscious minds will be on the same page, using the same information, and working towards the same goal of success and happiness. This is what you were born to do, this is what you desire, and this is what you will get if you follow the plan you create, work hard, and never give up. You are no different than any of the people whose cases have been reviewed in this work and can achieve the same results. Follow the outline provided and refer to the above case example for guidance.

What is your conscious awareness of what is happening?

1. Presenting issues-

2. Triggers to mood shift-

3. Thought process behind mood shift-

4. Resulting actions-

5. Outcome-

What are the belief systems your subconscious mind is operating with?

1. Origin experiences (Follow the outline of questions for history review)-

2. Parallels between your origin and present experiences-

3. Operating belief systems-

4. Changes needed-

Plan of correction:

1. Write down the negative belief systems you've been operating with and must now stop.

2. Write down the positive belief systems you want to operate with.

3. Write down the triggers that most strongly pull out your negative belief systems and moods.

4. Write down the cues and signals that tell you your negative belief systems are active.

5. Write down the positive responses to engage in when you realize you've been triggered.

a. What thought, image, word, or phrase will you use as a stop mechanism?

b. What is the positive self-talk you will use to dialogue with your subconscious to teach it to let go of the wrong information and accept the right information?

c. For each trigger, write down the positive perception of the event/situation/person that you want instead.

d. For each trigger, what is the positive mood you want to have about the situation/event/person?

e. For each trigger, what is the positive response and action you want to have instead?

f. Write down each in a goal statement that contains: When _____ happens, I will look at it _____way, choose to feel about it _____ way and respond to it _____ way, because my desired goal is _____. Review and repeat these action steps often.

6. Write down the method and schedule of delivery that you will use to flood your subconscious mind with your positive belief systems. Daily times you will meditate, do relaxation and visualization exercises, watch inspirational videos, set your cell phone alarm to prompt you to repeat your affirmations and goal statements, etc. Put your daily schedule up in sight and review daily. Whiteboards are great for this.

7. Write a list of positive activities you will use to create good experiences that will act as stress outlets and provide you with enjoyment. These will serve to reinforce the belief that you can do things to make yourself feel good. They will also be used to distract the mind and mood away from negative states.

8. Write down a goal list. Develop goals around here and now issues that are causing you anxiety and worry. Prioritize the list in order of importance. Start with goal number one and structure it like this:

I will complete _____ by this date_____ and here is how I will accomplish this.

     Step 1-

     Step 2-

     Step 3 and so on.

Mark off each step as it's completed and move onto the next. Move onto the next goal on your list after each one is accomplished. Put this goal up in sight and review it daily. Add the steps to your daily schedule. Add the goal statement to your daily repeated affirmation list. Tailor your visualization exercise to the goal.

9. Create the mechanisms for documenting and tracking your efforts and progress. Charts, graphs, journals, white boards, video documenting, notebooks, and any combination of these methods will work. Tracking progress alone will cause a person to progress towards their goal because it raises conscious awareness.

Remember to keep detailed notes as you move through this process. Ultimately, you want to have full knowledge and awareness of exactly what needs to be changed and how you're going to accomplish it. Documenting the process in written form helps your conscious mind to focus on the above goal and to identify only the essential information required. In the end, your written treatment plan should be simple, easily understood, and to the point. Once you start implementing your treatment plan, you should keep an ongoing written journal of your efforts so that you can analyze your progress. This will help pin point what is working, what isn't, and determine any adjustments that you need to make. It's important to understand that treatment is a process that is always unfolding and evolving. You start with a solid plan and then continue to improve on it as you go along. Eventually, you will arrive at what works best for you.

Chapter 8: The Tools

In previous chapters, relaxation exercises, meditation, and other cognitive techniques have been referenced as extremely valuable in facilitating the process of change. This chapter will focus on examining these tools in more detail and explaining how to use them.

The Exercises

1. The first is one of the most important, yet simplest, exercises to perform. It's a short relaxation exercise that focuses on breathing regulation. This exercise can be done almost anywhere and can be performed with the eyes open or closed. It can be done while engaged in an activity, or while lying down in a relaxed state. Simply focus on your breathing. If you don't have a cold, inhale the breath through the nostrils, very slowly. The key is to breathe in nice and slow and even and deep. Count to ten silently to regulate the cadence of the breath. Another key is to draw the breath through the diaphragm so that your abdomen expands first as you inhale. The bottom of the lungs will fill up first and then the top of the lungs, until the whole lung is filled. Have you ever noticed what happens to your breathing when you're extremely anxious or angry? The breathing becomes short, fast, choppy, and shallow through the top of the chest. This happens because the diaphragm tightens up so severely that the bottom of the lungs is restricted from expanding. The

breath will only go into the top of the lungs because the bottom is blocked off. With the breathing in such a state of dysregulation, a physiological chain reaction is quickly triggered. The heart rate directly follows the rate of breathing so the heart rate and blood pressure immediately skyrocket.

The important point being highlighted here is that the heart rate follows the breathing. By doing this exercise, the breathing rate slows down to about three breaths per minute which will cause the heart rate to slow down significantly. After inhaling the breath nice and slow and even, exhale it now at the same count of ten or even slower. This means you have to put the brakes on to insure it's released slowly. Repeat inhaling and exhaling the breath at this cadence until you feel your mind, mood, and body relaxing and slowing down which can happen within six to eight repetitions. This simple exercise only takes a few minutes and is very effective in calming the whole system down. I take my clients through this exercise in the very first session and advise them to start using it throughout their day. The ability to internally regulate the mind and mood is one of the most important skills to learn in life. This little exercise should be used every hour of the day. It's been repeatedly pointed out that the core problem that needs to be fixed is a belief system of fear that lies within the subconscious mind. This continual fear, that something bad is coming around the corner, plays like a broken record in the background of the mind and causes a person to live in a perpetual state of heightened anxiety.

Right from the start of treatment, it's important to get the conscious mind to play the opposite message throughout the day.

I have found that people living in this type of chronic fear and anxiety have a walking around state of at least five, with a lot of clients being seven or more when they first enter treatment. When the term walking around state is used, it's describing the lowest level of anxiety the person experiences. This is using the basic emotional pain scale of zero to ten, with ten being the worst, to measure the mood. Carrying around this level of anxiety indicates that the mind is working way too fast and hard. This state can be likened to an engine running at too many RPM's for too long. Eventually, parts of the engine will break down and the engine will stop running. The brain and the central nervous system can't sustain this level of stress. Problems will start surfacing with the executive functioning skills which involve concentration, short-term memory, tracking, sequencing, and organizing information. The mood, obviously, is severely distorted from the normal, healthy range of one to three. Additionally, perception becomes negatively altered as the senses are in a heightened state of alert, looking for trouble. As referred to earlier, this would be like wheeling a huge, six-foot magnifying glass in front of your eyes, turning little things into big problems.

The person is walking around in this heightened state, on the edge of their seat so to speak, watching and waiting for something bad to happen. If you've ever watched a really good horror movie, you'll have a good idea of the state of suspense being referred to here. As soon as the mind locks onto something that confirms its belief, the mood jumps quickly and severely. However, there is a great over reaction that occurs. This is because there is no tolerance space left. If a person is walking around at a seven or eight on the pain scale, it won't take much for them to jump to a ten. Conversely, a person walking around at a two or three has a lot of room left and it will take a whole lot more for them to leap to ten. Everyone has a cup inside and it holds only so much stress. Walking around every day with the fear created from past events fills the cup very close to its capacity and it will now only take something small for it to overflow.

This little exercise helps to reverse the process. The negative and false belief system is telling you to be afraid, to be very afraid. This fear is what holds the anxiety level so far up. Every time you do this exercise, you're telling yourself to be calm, to relax, and that everything's okay. You're steadily learning how to calm and soothe yourself. Again, repetition is the key. Over time, the consistent practice of breathing regulation will help to push the anxiety ceiling down. If you regularly use this exercise, and the others that will be outlined in this section, you will eventually retrain your brain, your mind, and your emotional structure. It will go back down to the normal, healthy range and you'll be able to hold it there.

At this time, it would be good to define what is being referred to as the healthy, normal range of the mood. In treatment, I have clients use the emotional pain scale to self-rate their mood. It's simple, effective, easy to use, and easy to understand. This helps people start to track their progress and to understand what the goal is in terms of where their mood should be on this scale at the end of treatment. Many clients enter treatment never having experienced a sustained, healthy mood state in their lives, especially if their troubles started in childhood. In fact, as noted previously, a very unhealthy, damaging mood range has been normalized, sometimes for decades. A lot of clients enter treatment with seven as their baseline normal, with frequent spiking to ten. Understandably, when people enter treatment, they want to get better quickly. They have been in so much emotional pain, for so long, that they want to be at zero and this is their goal. Complete freedom from any disturbance is the objective. However, this is an unrealistic goal and can lead to great frustration if they continue to define being fully emotionally healthy in this manner.

It's very important in treatment to help clients understand what a truly healthy mood state is and this simple scale puts this in very black and white terms. I explain immediately that when they are coming into session and rating their mood at under four on this scale for four consecutive weeks, the goal of treatment has been successfully achieved. It's now time to move into the maintenance and monitoring phase of treatment, which is once a month sessions for two to three months. If they continue to hold their mood in this range for this period of time, with very little contact, then treatment has been successfully completed. The illustrations at the end of the second chapter depict this scale with regards to the mood state of anxiety, which is the initial distortion of the mood when people first develop problems. Depression starts forming as a direct byproduct of a person living too long in a constant state of heightened anxiety, which is driven by the distorted negative belief system that something bad is about to happen and there's nothing they can do to stop it. When a client self-rates their mood below four for the time frame outlined above, this indicates that the quality of their thinking has become predominantly positive. As noted previously in this work, the mood exactly mirrors the thinking. At this point, they have successfully convinced their subconscious mind to let go of this negative belief system and replaced it with the positive one. They are no longer living in fear.

I tell clients, at the very beginning of treatment, that the healthy, normal mood state is one to three on this scale. I tell them that if you're alive and kicking, then you've got responsibilities and the natural worries that accompany them. This means that there's always going to be some level of anxiety going on internally, but it doesn't mean that the belief system is negative. This is just a normal part of being alive and moving through life. It's very important to understand this. If a person's goal is to live at zero on this scale, then they are going to be sadly disappointed when they can't sustain this. When I ask a client to rate their mood, I'm asking them about their general mood, which includes anxiety and anxiety's related states of anger and agitation. In addition, this rating will also include depression. The mood range of one to three indicates mild anxiety that is easily managed by the person's now strong and positive mind and causes no interference with their day to day functioning. This one to three range also indicates no depression and, conversely, the increased presence of happiness, joy, and peace in the mood. The goal of treatment is to make the mind so powerful that when legitimate problems do confront a person in life, they handle them effectively with no severe impact on the mood. There's no chance, whatsoever, that these events will turn the mind negative again. It's normal, during these times, for the mood to escalate to a five, six, or even seven, depending on what's occurring, but it won't stay there for long. The person's positive mindset kicks in quickly to meet the problem with the confidence to resolve it and then the mood will return back to the healthy range. This is what a healthy, resilient mood is like because it reflects a powerful mind. I tell clients that the zero on this scale is reserved for top of the mountain moments in life, we can and should visit there as often as possible, but we aren't going to live there and that's okay.

There is a second part to the above exercise. Once you feel yourself calmed down, let go of your focus on the breathing and it will stay nice and slow and even. At this point, silently repeat the positive affirmations you've created. As noted previously, these will be the polar opposite of the negative belief system you've identified that the subconscious mind needs to let go of. You need to create your own individual affirmations that are tailored to your own identified problem areas and the more detailed and specific, the better. As referred to before, the basic, overall, positive belief system you want integrated by your subconscious mind is this:

The world is a good place, with good people, and where good things happen. I have all the talent, skills, and abilities within me to be successful and happy.

This is a basic outline and can be used if you wish. However, I have found in treatment that each client ends up forming their own individual statements that are special to them and fit their own unique style. For example, people who are religious will often use scripture and prayers that have special meaning to them and say the same thing as the statement above. The idea is that you come up with this broader belief system in your own style, or use the one above and then add affirmations that are tailored to your own specific problem areas. For example, specific areas like in the case cited where the individual had to get his subconscious mind to accept as truth that driving was safe again. So, once you let go of focusing on the breathing, you should silently repeat, over and over, the broad belief system followed by your specific positive beliefs, affirmations, and goals. These should be repeated with deep concentration and conviction. This complete exercise takes no more than five minutes, but its effect is very powerful. The subconscious mind is listening to, and receiving, everything that you think about every day. Because it operates on pure repetition, it will eventually accept as truth whatever you repeatedly place into it enough times. This exercise gives you a method, and a structure, to drive in the new programming throughout the day. Use the alarm on your cell phone, or some other mechanism, to prompt yourself every hour to do this simple exercise. Without a reminder, you will forget.

This tool can also be used as part of the stop mechanism when you recognize that your mind has gone negative. As soon as your conscious mind becomes aware of the negative thinking, immediately picture a stop sign in your mind, then engage yourself in the breathing exercise and the positive self-talk. It's an effective way to switch the cognitive process from negative to positive. The more you do this exercise, the better you will get at it and the quicker your mind and mood will respond to it. Like any skill, continued practice develops increasing ability. You want to work on strongly conditioning the response so that your subconscious mind reacts to the command with growing speed. Again, this is all about the conscious mind regaining control and teaching the subconscious mind how to think, feel, and act for success. The goal is to line up the conscious and subconscious minds on the same page, operating with the right information, and with the conscious mind in the lead. The subconscious mind will follow the direction of the conscious mind if it demands it repeatedly enough. The repetitive process of denying the negative thought process and building the positive one promotes safety and security within the whole system, which ultimately removes fear and anxiety.

2. The next exercise is a longer version of the first and should be done once per day. This exercise takes more sustained concentration and needs to be done in a quiet place where you won't be disturbed. You should lie down or sit in a comfortable chair. Whatever you choose, it should be in a relaxed position where you have no pressure points on your body. These cause pain and will distract your concentration away from the exercise. This exercise is designed to relax your body and your mind to achieve a deeply calm state of mood. The primary goal, as it was in the first exercise, is to teach you how to independently and internally regulate your thought process and mood.

I have found that most people, especially in our society, don't even know that a wonderful place of healing exists within the mind. Most people, unfortunately, have one switch with two settings – on or off. There is no dimmer switch and no in between settings. Everyone is so busy with job, family, finances, and other responsibilities that they're running around, worried all day, and the mind is going way too fast. Some people will stay in this gear all day and their mind never slows down until the off switch is hit when they go to sleep. That is, if they can even fall asleep and stay asleep. All too often, at the end of the day, television, computers, video games, food, or drugs are used to slow the mind and mood down. Sadly, most people in our society have never experienced what being truly relaxed and calm is, and that this place can be accessed within their own mind.

It's very important, in the development of mental and emotional well-being, to learn where this place is in the mind and dive down into it daily. This exercise shows you that it does exist and how to get there. It shows that you can induce a very positive and wonderfully relaxed state by using only your mind. The effects of this exercise, and any like it, are truly wide ranging. It improves memory, concentration, all of the executive functioning skills, and the mood. There is a hangover effect on the mood where it will remain in a state of calm sometimes several hours after the exercise has been completed. The exercise can also be used as a sleep inducer by doing it just before going to bed. Like the first exercise, it has the primary effect of reducing the walking around state of fear and anxiety that a person carries within them. In addition, it reinforces the positive belief system that good things do happen and you have the ability to make them happen. Here is the exercise:

Relaxation/Empowerment Exercise

As we begin, let your body settle comfortably into the chair that you're sitting in. Just let your body start to relax and let go of all that stored up tension. This is a time to leave all your worries behind and dive down into your mind where there exists a wonderful place of healing that will calm you, rejuvenate you, and strengthen you. I'm going to read you this script and all you have to do is relax and follow it along. Keep your eyes open as the exercise begins.

Look straight ahead and pick out one spot, and then stare at that spot without moving a muscle. Now, take in a deep breath and fill up your lungs, and then exhale that breath slowly. Take in a second and even deeper breath, take in all the air that your lungs can hold, and then exhale that breath slowly. And just start relaxing even more. At this time, you can close your eyes. Keep them closed until the end of the exercise, and I'll ask you to open them again.

In your mind's eye, I want you to imagine you're looking at the tips of the toes of your feet. Picture a wave of relaxation flowing from your toes all the way back into your heels, and mentally turn all those muscles loose. As your feet relax, allow your mind to relax, too. Feel your mind unwinding and letting go of all your worries, tensions, and anxieties. And now, imagine this wave of relaxation flowing on up into your ankles, and then all the way up to your knees. Picture your calf muscles becoming loose and relaxed. Your breathing continues to remain calm and smooth. With each breath you take in, you can feel yourself drifting deeper and deeper into drowsy relaxation. In fact, you're breathing just as you do each night, when you're deep and sound asleep. Now, let this wave of relaxation flow on up from your knees, and all the way up to your hips. As it touches each part of your thighs, picture all the muscles growing loose and limp, heavy and so relaxed.

Now, let this wave of relaxation flow on up into the muscles of your abdomen, and into your whole stomach area. A lot of tension is usually stored in this part of the body. As the wave moves gently into this area, picture all the stored up tension being washed away, leaving the muscles loose and relaxed. And now, as those muscles relax, just continue to allow your mind to relax, too. Let it float off to enjoy happy and pleasant scenes in your imagination. As your mind continues to drift deeper and deeper into a state of soothing relaxation, imagine the wave flowing up through your ribcage, into your lungs, and all the way up into the muscles of your chest. You can feel this whole area of your body calming, relaxing, and just letting go. Your breathing continues to remain nice and slow and even, just as it does each night when you're deep and sound asleep. As a result, your heart beats at the same nice and slow and even pace, which causes you to be carried even deeper into drowsy relaxation.

Now, picture this wave of relaxation flowing on up into your neck, and feel all the muscles around your neck growing loose and relaxed. Imagine the wave now moving from the back of your neck and spiraling all the way down through the muscles along your spine. As it touches each area of your spine, all the stored up tension is released and the muscles become heavy and so relaxed. As those muscles unwind, you continue to drift deeper and deeper into a state of wonderful relaxation. And now, picture this wave of relaxation spreading out from each side of your spine and into the rest of the broad muscles of your back.

Now, picture the wave flowing up into your upper back and shoulder muscles. This is another area of the body that usually stores a lot of tension. Just imagine all these muscles smoothing out and relaxing as soon as the comforting wave rolls into them. And, as those muscles relax, just continue to allow your mind to relax, too. Let your mind drift off to happy and pleasant scenes in your imagination. Now, picture this wave of relaxation splitting into two and flowing from the shoulders, down through the arms, and all the way to the fingertips of both hands. As the waves move into each muscle, you can feel all the muscles of the arms, hands, and fingers growing loose and limp, heavy and so relaxed. As those muscles unwind, you continue to drift deeper and deeper into drowsy relaxation.

Now, picture this wave of relaxation flowing up into your jaws, and then moving gently through all the muscles of your face. Just imagine the calming wave circling around your mouth, moving up through your nose, and all around your eyes. Continue to picture it flowing across your forehead, down around your temples, and then back around your ears. As this wave of relaxation touches each muscle, you can feel all the tension in your face being released. And finally, imagine it moving from your ears and spreading out to the back of your neck, and all the way up to the top of your skull.

At this time, your entire body is being bathed in the pleasant glow of complete and utter relaxation. Each muscle, from the tips of your toes to the top of your head, is loose, limp, and relaxed, and you feel so good.

Continue to hold onto this feeling of soothing relaxation. Just imagine that you're floating in a pool of healing waters, with gentle waves of light, warmth, and peace surrounding you and supporting you. Completely content and secure, not a care in the world, just floating. As you calmly float along, you can feel a growing sense of peace, love and strength building within you.

Now, as you continue to bathe in this wonderful state of healing and relaxation, we will reinforce the growing power within you.

Today, I will have a great day. No matter what happens around me, I will maintain a positive attitude.

I have all the talents, skills, and abilities within me to achieve whatever I set my mind to. The keys to my success and happiness already lie within me.

I will always move forward whenever confronted by any obstacle. I look at all obstacles as opportunities to grow stronger, better, and to acquire new skills. I believe that I have the ability to overcome any obstacle that faces me.

I am too large for worry, too noble for anger, too strong for fear, and too happy to permit the presence of trouble in my life.

I am powerful, worthy, valuable, and good. I choose to focus on all the good that exists around me and in all the people I come in contact with each day. I am so strong and positive that negativity can't live within me.

I release my negative past so that I am free to pursue the positive future of my choosing. I refuse to allow the negative situations and people of my past to dictate how I think, feel, and act any longer.

And now, the exercise is over. You can simply open your eyes and you will continue to feel wonderfully relaxed and empowered.

Exercise End

Either in place of the positive affirmations, or at the end of them, you can insert the visualization of targeted goals. This is the exact exercise I have used with clients for the past twenty years. I take them through it during a session and explain its importance and impact. I then advise them to go on YouTube, or in the apps section on their cell phones, and find a guided relaxation or meditation exercise that follows this one as closely as possible. However, I have had some clients use relaxing sounds, including music, to achieve the same tranquil mental and emotional state that this exercise does. Again, I like clients to find what works for them outside of our sessions so that they own it. I have had some clients copy this script and have someone read it at home, or they tape record it so that they can use it by themselves. Either way, the eventual goal is to memorize whatever is used until they can run it through their mind without any external narration.

Most clients are able to achieve a very calm state on the first attempt, despite the heightened state of anxiety they're in. Others, because of more severe fear and anxiety, find their concentration wavers too much and they're too easily distracted. I always tell them that this doesn't mean it won't work for them, or that it was a failure. It just shows how much anxiety they have running through them and how important it is that they work on learning how to control their mood. If they continue to practice daily and don't give up, their mind will respond and they will inevitably achieve the desired goal of the exercise. As noted earlier, the more you practice, the better you get at it. Whenever clients have a successful response to the exercise, I show them the paper and tell them that these are just words on paper. It was their mind that created the peaceful and calm state that they just experienced. The words are mere suggestion, and mean nothing unless the mind buys into it and gets the body and mood to respond accordingly.

3. The third exercise is a variation of the first two. It's specifically designed to condition a word, mental image, or phrase directly to a happy and calm mood state. You can

use either the first or second exercise to bring yourself down into a calm state. In the fourth paragraph of the above exercise, there is a line that asks you to drift off to happy and pleasant scenes in your imagination. When you get to the end of whichever exercise you choose, focus your mind on a time in your life when you were really happy. Let your mind wander over this and images will start coming into your mind. The first image that comes into your mind will usually be the one that holds the most power in your mind. The idea now is to hold whatever comes up in your mind's eye. Whether it's a word, object, image, or phrase, focus your concentration on holding onto that image and trying to visualize it in increasing detail. In addition, focus on bringing up the feeling connected with that vision. Work on immersing yourself in that feeling of joy and happiness. Whenever your mind wanders to another thought, bring it back immediately to focus on the vision. Really work hard on producing the emotion connected to it and holding onto it.

One of my past clients had an apple come up into his mind while going through his first exposure to the second exercise listed. When I read the line that states, drift off to happy and pleasant scenes in your imagination, an apple popped into his mind. At first, he was confused by this, but while driving home from the session, he realized that the apple was connected to a crabapple tree that was in his childhood backyard. That tree was the center of many fun times with his siblings and friends growing up. The apple that came into his mind was a symbol of great happiness for him. Powerful and positive emotions were directly tied to its image. He used this exercise to strengthen the bond even more intensely and found that whenever he became upset during his day (he was a medical doctor and experienced tremendous stress), he would place the apple in his mind and the distressed mood would melt away into happiness. He stated, during his last session before ending treatment, that it had become a great source of strength for him in his life. This is the goal of the exercise and it can be achieved by anyone if practiced hard enough. The subconscious mind operates on pure repetition and it will accept, as a truth, anything that is repeated often enough into it. The goal of this exercise is to condition powerful, positive emotions directly to a mental image so strongly, that placing it into the mind will immediately wipe out any negative emotional state that has attempted to take it over.

4. Another simple mental exercise is using a running list of all the good things that are going on in your life. When the mind and mood are predominantly negative, nothing looks good in life and almost everything becomes dark. The mind tends to focus on only the bad things and the good things are forgotten, pushed aside, or even turned into negatives. Write down everything you can think of and nothing is too small. Things like having food to eat, running water, shelter, clothes to wear, a bed to sleep in, etc. You get the idea. Keep this list out in the open and add to it every time you think of something else that isn't on there already. The goal here is to overwhelm the subconscious

mind with the sheer numbers of this information and the truth that not everything is bad. When you have several pages written out, you want to spread them out so they take up as much visual space as possible and then read them. By doing this, you're giving your subconscious mind actual visual evidence that there are a lot of good things going on in your life. In fact, many more good things than bad. This directly counters the negative belief system you're working on getting rid of and reinforces the positive one that you're convincing the subconscious mind to integrate in its place. After you get done reading it, close your eyes and silently churn in your mind that positive belief system:

Good things happen in this world and they're happening to me and I can continue to make more good things happen in my life.

A similar version of this exercise can be used at the end of each day. At some point in the evening before going to bed, write down all the good and positive events that happened during your day. After completing the list, read it over again and then reflect on how productive the day was and how tomorrow is going to be the same way. This is another effective tool to help teach the mind how to concentrate and think in positive terms about your life.

5. The fifth exercise is to write down your empowerment statements and positive belief systems and put them up multiple places so that you can't help but run into them throughout your day. Tape one to your bathroom mirror

so you see it when you get ready in the morning. Put one by the door so you see it every time you leave the house. Place another one in your car so you see it every time you drive. Put one on your work station so you see it throughout your work day. Tape one on the refrigerator so you see it every time you open the refrigerator door. As I mentioned previously, I have had clients put one on the ceiling over their bed so it's the first thing they see in the morning and the last thing they see before they go to bed at night. When you look at each of your statements, pause and read it silently, or out loud, with great conviction, emotion, and belief. Again, repetition is the key. The more you flood your mind with these positive messages, the faster your subconscious mind will lock onto these and believe them to be true.

6. The next exercise is specifically designed to get the subconscious mind to release injury that is connected with people from the past. I recommend this method for clients who continue to carry around anger and hate towards individuals in their past that hurt them badly. Most often, this occurs in relationships with powerful people like parents or romantic relationships. We have previously discussed how the subconscious mind will use any resource at its disposal to continue to recreate unresolved issues from past failed relationships. Continuing to carry around anger, rage, and hate towards people that have hurt us only serves to pollute the mind and the body with poison. It also will cause us to be drawn repeatedly back into abusive relationships with people who closely

resemble these figures from the past, which only increases the anger and hate that is internalized. This is why it's so important to convince the subconscious mind to let go of the past so it doesn't interfere with our lives anymore.

Years ago, I had a client enter treatment who was sexually abused by her father repeatedly when she was a child. Understandably, she continued to hold tremendous anger and hate towards him. Most victims of this type of abuse don't feel that they can confront the perpetrator and never have a chance to release their anger like they want to, or even fantasize about. This is especially true when the perpetrator is a parental figure, and was no different in her case. This client came to treatment about a year after her father passed away. As often happens, the perpetrator's death triggers a tremendous emotional reaction where the anger and hate are intensified. Severe depression can soon follow if this intense mental and emotional state isn't relieved. Her mood became increasingly destabilized and she was starting to have trouble functioning in her day to day life. The death of her father caused the abuse of her past to explode to the surface and her mind became overwhelmed with the memories of the abuse.

As part of her treatment, I suggested she write a letter to her father. I advised her that the letter should reflect the raw emotion that was inside of her and to use words that captured just how she felt about him. I told her not to edit the letter and that it should contain her real thoughts and feelings. I asked her to write the letter as if her father was standing right in front of her. This was an opportunity for her to say and do all the things she had ever wanted. At the end of the letter, I instructed her that the last part should contain a statement that she was letting this part of her past go and she wasn't going to allow him to hurt her anymore. She was renouncing the anger and hate of his abuse so she could freely move forward into the future.

When the letter was done, the next step was to read it out loud to someone she trusted. This could be done in session, or with someone else close to her in her life. She chose to read the letter in session. Both writing and reading the letter usually evokes a tremendous emotional release. This is one of the primary purposes of this exercise. It gives long buried memories and powerful emotions a tangible form outside of the person. Writing is perfect for this. After she read the letter, the next step was to create a ceremonial gesture that signified and symbolized releasing her father and the past connected to him. I tell clients that they can do whatever they like, but it should be destroyed. Burning these letters is the most popular method that people choose. The last step is to read it out loud one last time and destroy it while repeating any version of the affirmation: "I release my past so that I can look forward to my future." This is a very powerful action and message to the subconscious mind to let go of it because it's done, it's over, and has no significance anymore. The client I'm referring to didn't burn hers. Rather, she stood over her father's grave, read it to him, and then buried it at his grave site. In the next session after this final act, she reported that the experience had been very powerful and, immediately afterwards, felt like a huge weight had been lifted from her. From that moment on, her mind stopped obsessing on the past abuse, her mood improved dramatically, and her daily functioning returned to normal. Her subconscious mind had gotten the message and she was finally freed from her abuser.

7. The seventh exercise is meditation. Once you get good at the second or third exercise, it's time to start incorporating meditation which should be done once per day. Use a timer and set it for five minutes. I recommend that meditation should be done sitting upright in a chair, or on the edge of the bed. I don't recommend doing it while lying down on a bed, or on a recliner. It's too easy to fall asleep in these positions, especially if you're meditating at the end of the day and you're tired. Next, you want to pick out an anchor to be used in the mind. If you've been practicing the third exercise, you can use the same image as your anchor. Again, this anchor can be a word, image, object, scene, phrase, prayer, or even the absence of thought. It doesn't matter what it is, but should be something that your mind can grasp and focus on fairly easily. Set the timer, close your eyes, and then place the anchor into your mind and hold it. For most people, the mind will wander off onto another thought within five to ten seconds. As soon as you realize your mind has moved off the anchor, return it back to the anchor. Repeat this

process, over and over again, during the five minutes. When the timer goes off, this is the end of the meditation session.

The goal, every time you meditate, is to hold your concentration on the anchor for longer and longer periods of time. This will happen naturally with continued practice. When you can hold your mind on the anchor without it wandering much during the five minutes, increase the limit to ten minutes. Add five minutes every time your power of concentration grows and is sustained without much wandering. When you can sustain your concentration for thirty minutes, with very few distractions away from the anchor, you will have completed a truly great feat. It's very hard to sustain this level of concentration for one minute, let alone thirty minutes. What's the benefit of this exercise? The bottom line is that it increases thought control. This is the core skill that needs to be developed to permanently remove any bad habit and replace it with a new, positive one. The basis of change is the ability to consciously identify negative thinking as soon as possible, stop it, and then redirect the mind to positive thinking. The stronger your ability to control your thoughts, the more successful you will be with this. Quite simply, there's nothing better than meditation to build this skill. However, it's the hardest exercise listed here and takes time and patience to build the ability. But, if you stick with it, you'll get better and better at it.

8. Lastly, these are some additional exercises and activities suggested to help improve the ability to sustain concentration. The old concentration card game that you may have played as a child is still one of the best. The first time you play it, start out with eight to ten matching pairs and keep adding pairs until you reach a number of cards that really challenges your ability. Keep track of the time it takes to successfully match all the pairs and try to improve your best time each time you play the game. Increase the number of pairs when the current number of cards you're using isn't challenging enough.

The next exercise involves using a box of crayons. Start with four different colors and make colored circles on a piece of paper all in a row. Make sure to scramble the crayons so they're not in the same order on the table top when you put them back down. Study the order of the colors for about twenty to thirty seconds and then cover the colored circles. Now, reproduce the exact order of the colors and then check the original order for accuracy. Increase the number of colors until you reach a number that becomes difficult. Continue at this number until you build your powers of concentration and are successful again. Try to increase the amount of colors whenever you can. This same exercise can also be done with sequences of numbers, letters, and words.

Another method for improving concentration and memory retention is to read and then produce a written summary of the content. Select material that you enjoy reading in the form of a book, magazine, newspaper article, etc. Start with smaller sections and then build your way up to larger sections of what you're reading. For example, if it's a book, begin with a page or two and then immediately summarize it without referring back to the book. When this amount of information no longer presents a challenge, increase the volume to three to four pages. Gradually work your way up to a full chapter with an eventual goal of reading an entire book and then writing a detailed summary afterwards. I have often recommended this exercise for students who want to improve academic ability. In addition, all of the listed exercises are excellent for children and adults with attention deficit disorder.

Play any board or card games that involve strategy. Learn how to play chess. Learn a language. Learn to play a musical instrument. Learn to paint or sculpt. Build models, do crossword puzzles, etc. Regular involvement in any of these activities will strengthen the quality of the mind.

Restructuring the Mood

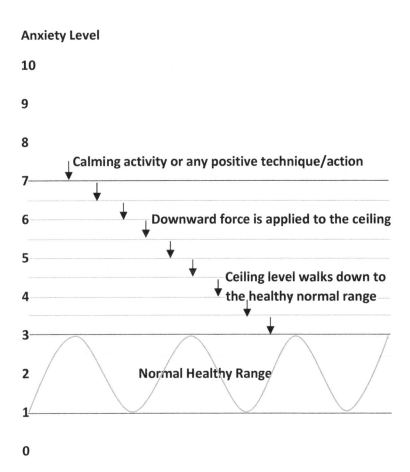

Anxiety Level

Calming activity or any positive technique/action

Downward force is applied to the ceiling

Ceiling level walks down to the healthy normal range

Normal Healthy Range

Repeatedly challenging any fear based belief system, and not allowing it to run unchecked in the mind, will create a positive mood structure.

Epilogue: Keep the Conscious Mind in Charge

The overall goal is to make the mind live increasingly in the positive and decreasingly in the negative. The exercises outlined in the previous chapter are some very good examples of techniques that cultivate positive mental and emotional states and help to sustain them. Again, I encourage you to create your own style, adapt and adjust them to how you think they will help you the best. Augment with inspirational videos, music, books, and movies. Supplement with exercise, crafts, hobbies, good friends, and any positive activities you like and enjoy. When you're engaged in these types of activities, your mind and mood are in a positive state.

Watch who you associate with because, as mentioned before, your brain will resonate at the same frequency as the brains and environment around you. If you hang around negative people, and in negative environments long enough, you will start thinking and acting just like they do. Make sure the people and environments you choose to be around are positive. This is hard for most people because what happens is that, as the quality of their mind improves and becomes increasingly positive, they start analyzing the faces and places in their life in the same manner as their own thinking. They start realizing that a good percentage of the people they hang around with, and the places they frequent, are negative influences that were put there by their old, negative mind. Even the person's current job will be called into question. With their mind becoming progressively positive, they find that their new mind no longer lines up with friends, environments, and even family members. They become increasingly uncomfortable with them, and are faced with the growing need to make changes to keep their mind growing in a positive direction. This can call for some hard choices, but ones that have to be made.

Once these negative influences are recognized, don't be afraid to make the necessary changes. The continued development of the positive quality of your mind, mood, and your life depends on it. Choose to be around positive, powerful, and strong people because this is how you want to be. If you've identified that your job is holding you back and is a negative influence, don't be afraid to change it and believe that you can. The same goes for relationships. Become so strong and positive that negativity can't live inside or outside of you because you won't permit it.

If you follow the concepts, process, and techniques outlined in this work, your conscious mind will become fully awakened and capable of doing the job it was designed to do. Its job is to demand that the subconscious mind operates with the right belief systems so that you can be successful and happy. If you persevere, don't give up, and continue to work hard, it's inevitable that you will get stronger and stronger. However, I want to add a word of caution. You will get better to the point where you think that you've reached your goals and your work is done.

Don't ever believe this. This is the negative mind trying to win you back again.

The work does get easier, but never stop doing the things that brought you progress and success. The methods and techniques you used have to be incorporated as part of your lifestyle, for the rest of your life. I always warn my clients in treatment about this natural human tendency to relax once we think we've got it conquered. Treating the mind isn't like taking a course of antibiotics for a bodily infection. Once you've finished the medicine, the infection is gone, and the medication doesn't have to be continued to keep it from coming back. With the mind, if you don't maintain conscious vigilance and the cognitive techniques that have been outlined, negative belief systems will start to grow. The subconscious mind will go off on its own again with the wrong information and the problems will return. It's important to understand that the negative mind isn't gone, but has been weakened to the point where it has sunk to the bottom of the subconscious mind where it has no influence anymore. However, if fed again, it will wake up and intensify its efforts to regain control over your mind. The conscious mind must be kept activated so that the positive mind stays awake and strong, and the negative mind stays asleep and weak.

At the end of treatment, the goal is to maintain and to further build the quality of the mind that has been achieved. The vulnerability at this point, which can cause the conscious mind to be lulled back to sleep, is the false sense that the work is done. In the beginning of treatment, the way the negative mind tries to get you to give up is much different. I always show clients a progress graph which helps to understand that the natural pace of progress is never linear. Progress is always two steps forward, one back, or even one step forward, and two back. People who are engaged in physical therapy for a bodily injury know this process all too well. When those back steps occur, it can cause great disappointment and discouragement. This is when people are at risk of giving up the fight because they feel that they are back at the beginning and haven't made any progress at all. This is when the negative mind will work very hard in order to convince them that what they're doing isn't working, so why keep doing it? However, this is yet another deception.

Take a look at the progress graph that's at the end of this chapter. If you focus just on the valleys that are marked with a star on this graph, they all look the same as the one at the starting point. But if you step back and look at the whole graph, it's easy to see that the points of downturn in progress aren't anywhere near the beginning. Looking at the whole picture clearly reveals that a lot of progress has been made. It's just a temporary stop in progress that will be ended by not listening to the negative voice and working harder than before. If the person handles it the right way, a new level of progress will be achieved. The point behind these examples of how the negative mind will look for any advantage to regain control, is to never allow the conscious mind to fall away from its job as the controller of your mind. Once awakened, keep the conscious mind awake, active, and vigilant. If you do this, you'll never return to a life of misery again. For the rest of your life, you will continue to grow in confidence, success, and happiness. Always remember that it's not the negative events in life that cause the real problems to occur. Rather, the actual difficulties are created by letting these experiences turn your mind negative. Never, ever, allow anyone or any situation to make you think badly about yourself or your life, and don't ever forget that you have a choice in this. How you choose to think about the adverse events in your life is what will ultimately determine the quality of your life. This applies to both past and present events, as well as any that are negatively predicted for the future. Regularly review the following flow chart to reinforce this concept:

1. Negative event/situation

2. Thought process= What do I think about it? **This choice determines everything that follows.**

3. Mood= How do I feel about it?

4. Action= What am I going to do about it?

5. Outcome= What is the eventual impact on me?

Regardless of the situation, positive responses with the thought process will result in positive moods, actions, and outcomes. Negative responses will only deliver negative moods, actions, and outcomes. This is why it's so critical that your primary focus in life should always be on improving your own mind. Hold on strongly to this great truth:

The quality of your life is generated solely by the quality of your thinking.

Think of your subconscious mind as the garden and your conscious mind as the gardener. If the gardener doesn't go out every day and tend to the garden, what happens? The garden becomes overgrown with weeds that eventually choke out and kill all the good plants in the garden. The gardener must pull those weeds and put weed killer down to prevent them from growing again. To grow strong, the good plants need to be fertilized, fed, and watered. The gardener must work hard every day to insure that the garden is successful and bears lots of delicious vegetables, fruits, and beautiful flowers. Make sure to tend to your garden every day and you will cultivate a beautiful life.

I wish you strength and courage in your journey, and I hope that the information contained in this work brings you peace, success, and happiness.

Progress Graph

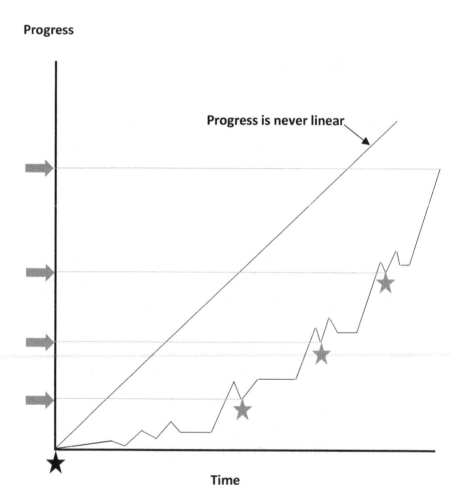

These setbacks can look like there has been no progress from the beginning. Many people give up at these times.

However, when you step back and look at the whole picture, huge progress is being made.

Some additional guidelines for help:

If you ever experience suicidal ideation, inform a trusted family member or friend immediately. Seek their help and support. Don't try to handle this on your own, or through drugs or alcohol. The depression and suicidal ideation will only intensify. Have your support person take you immediately to the nearest hospital emergency room for evaluation. If you don't have a trusted support person, or they aren't available at the time, call the National Suicide Prevention Lifeline at 1-800-273-8255, or contact 911 for help.

If you are experiencing severe depression, anxiety, or mood swings, contact your primary care doctor and make an appointment to talk with him or her about your symptoms. Your doctor can refer you to a mental health provider. If you have insurance, contact them and find out which mental health providers are covered by your insurance and make an appointment. If you don't have insurance, contact your county's community mental health access center to initiate mental health services.

This work has been constructed to act as a self-help manual. However, you can look for a psychotherapist who is trained in Cognitive Behavioral Therapy (CBT) and ask them if they can support you in following the treatment process outlined in this book. Mental health treatment, especially in large health systems, has moved towards Person Centered Planning which means that providers will incorporate what you want to accomplish in your treatment plan. A psychotherapist, skilled in CBT, would be able to review this work and help you implement the treatment process.

Made in the USA
Monee, IL
28 March 2022

93695911R00098